Toward a New Theory of Architecture

RUDOLF STEINER (1914)

Toward a New Theory of Architecture

THE FIRST GOETHEANUM IN PICTURES

An introductory lecture with slides
Given in Bern, Switzerland, June 29, 1921

EDITED AND TRANSLATED BY FREDERICK AMRINE
INTRODUCTION BY JOHN KETTLE

Rudolf Steiner

SteinerBooks

CW 290

We would like to thank the Provost's Office, the College of Literature, Science, and the Arts, and the Department of Germanic Languages and Literatures at the University of Michigan for their generous publication subsidy.

Copyright © 2017 by SteinerBooks

SteinerBooks | Anthroposophic Press
610 Main Street
Great Barrington, Massachusetts 01230
www.steinerbooks.org

Original translation from German by Frederick Amrine

This book is volume 290 in the Collected Works (CW) of Rudolf Steiner, published by SteinerBooks 2017. Translated from the 3rd revised German edition, *Das Goetheanum als Gesamtkunstwerk: Rudolf Steiner, Der Baugedanke des Goetheanum: Einleitender Vortrag mit Erklärungen zu den Lichtbildern des Goetheanum-Baues gehalten in Bern am 29. Juni 1921*, edited by Walther Roggenkamp, Dornach, Verlag am Goetheanum, 1986.

Print: 978-1-62148-097-6
e-Book: 978-1-62148-098-3

Printed in the United States of America

CONTENTS

INTRODUCTION

The Architecture of the Future

BY JOHN KETTLE

SCARCELY A SOUL NOW REMAINS ON EARTH who can have seen the startlingly original first Goetheanum building, who can have known its overwhelming beauty, who can have experienced what Rudolf Steiner called the living language of its forms. So it remains to this book to try at least to suggest what the building must have been to those who were there in the few years the building stood.

The foundation stone of the building was laid in the village of Dornach, near the city of Basel in Switzerland, more than a century ago, on September 20, 1913. Within a year the First World War broke out, but the work of construction continued. In 1920, the almost-completed building was formally opened. A year later, at the end of June 1921, in the Swiss city of Bern, Steiner gave the slide lecture that is this book's chief content. Just eighteen months after that, the still incomplete building was destroyed by fire.

The Genesis of the First Goetheanum

As one's eyes scan every form and line of this great structure, it becomes apparent that the Goetheanum is unique. The German architectural historian Wolfgang Pehnt noted, "Steiner's creations are perplexing, for they stand in virtual isolation … they scarcely show any recognizable origins, and they established no tradition except within the Anthroposophical movement itself." He further wrote: "the fundamental architectural concept of the *Johannesbau* [the unbuilt forerunner of the Goetheanum, designed in 1908 to be erected in Munich], the interpenetration of two domed rooms of different sizes, and many of the details, are without parallel."[1]

The need for the Goetheanum can be traced back to Steiner's work in Munich, beginning in 1907. A building was required to house the courses and lectures that Steiner was giving there. "[O]nly an interior structure was specifically envisioned, because it would be surrounded by several houses, occupied by friends who could settle there," Steiner recalled. The building and its surrounding of three-, four-, and five-story houses would have occupied a city block in the suburb of Schwabing. "After great difficulty in the arrangements for building on the site already acquired in Munich, we discovered that we were opposed, not only by the police or local authorities, but by the Munich Society of Arts. Indeed, it was done in such a way that we felt our establishment in Munich was objected to by these worthy individuals."[2]

The need for a theater or lecture hall was not all that inspired Steiner and the theosophists in Munich, though. According to Hella Wiesberger, "That the idea for building a temple stood in the background of the Munich [Theosophical Congress of 1907] was not just implied by the capital forms in the columns that Steiner created. The connection is also explicit in a letter that Marie von Sivers wrote to Edouard Schuré, whose reconstruction of the *Sacred Drama of Eleusis* was premiered at the Munich Congress. She wrote: 'With that, we can try to approach the idea of a temple'."[3] The prospect of creating some sort of religious or secular cathedral was vivid in the minds of Expressionist architects in the days following the devastation of Europe in the First World War. "Painters and sculptors, break through the barriers to architecture and become fellow builders, fellow strugglers for the final goal of art: the creative conception of the cathedral of the future, which will once again be all in one shape, architecture and sculpture and painting," Walter Gropius wrote in a leaflet for an Exhibition for Unknown Architects to be held in Berlin in April 1919. The words closely corresponded to his manifesto announcing the opening of the Bauhaus, which came later that year.[4] Much the same thought lay behind the German architect Bruno Taut's idea of building a secular cathedral in every city.[5]

Steiner makes it clear in his lecture, though, that he did not intend the Goetheanum to be a temple, but rather a step forward—as a place where "from the other side, [those within] receive communications that provide knowledge of higher worlds," adding that to describe the building as a temple reflected "an inability to find new words for new experiences." Nevertheless, the Goetheanum continued to be described as a temple or cathedral, not entirely, perhaps, but certainly in part because of the expectation that new architectural movements must eventually produce such buildings.

The Society's impasse in Munich was solved when a Swiss anthroposophist, Dr. Emil Grosheintz, offered the Society a large tract of land in Dornach. The land itself, the surrounding Jura Mountains in particular, so different from the Munich suburb in which the Goetheanum had originally been intended to stand, had a definite effect on its design. A major feature, the roof line, was significantly softened. When construction started, the work was carried out by hundreds of people, both men and women, from at least seventeen different countries.[6] There are fine photographs of the building under construction that show women as well as men involved in the heavy work such as carving the building's capitals. The devotion of all the workers was extraordinary; people who were there found it almost overwhelming. Some likened it to another Pentecost miracle.[7]

There is no doubt that Steiner was an architect of extraordinary achievement in his own right. "The major buildings erected at Dornach before his death in 1925 are rightly attributed to him, rather than to the particular architect who carried out the work," Pehnt has noted.[8] "Steiner conveyed his plastic and architectural ideas in a variety of ways—through verbal instructions, sketches and models, data concerning plans and dimensions, practical work on the site and in the workshops, and lastly through the famous Dornach *Doktor-Korrekturen* [Doctor corrections] at which he made improvements to his colleagues' designs." Some notion of Steiner's approach to design may be gathered from an aspect of the design of the building's two interlocking cupolas. These cupolas were the upper parts of two spheres, the larger set above the auditorium, the smaller above the stage. In Steiner's initial design the larger of the spheres was meant to encompass and express the building's physical aspect while the smaller would encompass its spiritual aspects. Steiner originally envisaged that the larger sphere would rest on the auditorium floor, while the bottom of the smaller, spiritual sphere would float several meters above the stage floor.[9]

Speaking as an architect, Steiner nowhere talks of inspiration from the past or from his contemporaries; rather, he says that "whatever objections may still be raised against this style of architecture, it is nevertheless the style and the architecture of the future."[10,11] He saw his own architectural impulse on an historical or epochal scale. In several lectures he described the great phases in the development of architectural form: "The god dwelt in the Greek temple, the spirit of the congregation can dwell in the Romanesque or Gothic building, but in the architecture of the future the spiritual world is meant to *speak*."[12]

Nonetheless, Steiner was intensely aware of what was going on in the world around him, in politics, in the economy, in society, and in art; in turn he exerted a considerable influence on contemporary art and architecture. He was connected with the Theosophical Society from 1900, when he gave his first lectures in the theosophical library in Berlin. The connection was at first close, then gradually less so, until in 1912 he finally detached himself from the Theosophical Society and formed the Anthroposophical Society. In these years theosophy had attracted the attention and often the devotion of many artists. In his mid-thirties the Dutch painter Piet Mondrian became interested in theosophy and then anthroposophy (though it would be hard to find much evidence of this in his painting). Wassily Kandinsky, the Russian painter, who lived in Munich when he and Franz Marc founded the Blue Rider group, took much of his approach from theosophical and anthroposophical ideas. Steiner's work in Munich at that time included the writing and staging of his own Mystery Dramas.[13] In 1910, the year the first of these Mystery Dramas was staged, Kandinsky's first abstract watercolor was painted. Two years later his design for the cover of the *Blaue Reiter* almanac, which gave its name to the art movement led by Kandinsky and Marc, coincided with Steiner's third Mystery Drama. Two years further on, Kandinsky's work had become completely abstract. Franz Marc, Kandinsky's colleague in the *Blaue Reiter* movement, also worked his way from representational painting, for example *The Blue Horses*, to abstraction in the years 1911-13.

Many writers on the art movements of the early twentieth century have found a link between new urges and artists' interest in theosophy and anthroposophy. Many prominent artists—James Joyce, Arnold Schönberg, the Italian Futurists, etc.—were influenced by theosophy in the early part of the twentieth century. Michael Howard, a sculptor and teacher, has written: "Rudolf Steiner's views and practice of art are intimately united with the impulses that have arisen in the souls of many artists of his time. It must be noted that Steiner's own artistic work (from 1907 until 1924) was contemporary with, and sometimes influential in shaping, the development of some significant artists—most notably, Wassily Kandinsky."[14] Thomas Steinfeld goes further: "A large part of modernism in the visual arts, music, literature and architecture was inspired by theosophy."[15] Behind this lay a growing despair at Europe's increasingly oppressive trend toward materialism and the search for a way to counter it—an "outcry against materialism, against anti-mind, against the machine, against centralization, for mind, for God, for the human in man," as a contemporary put it.[16] Peter Fingesten, the Berlin-born Surrealist painter who moved to the U. S. in 1939 and eventually became chair of Pace University's art department, wrote: "[W]hat some choose to see today in terms of pure aesthetics, was to Mondrian (and Kandinsky as well) an expression of pure spirit."[17]

Kandinsky's development as an artist was deeply influenced by his familiarity with Steiner as a lecturer and writer, and Steiner's profound insight into the nature of art. "When in 1910 Wassily Kandinsky wrote *Concerning the Spiritual in Art*—his artistic manifesto—he mentioned theosophy not only as his main fellow combatant against a world that was far too materialistic but also as the messenger of a 'new form of expression,' accorded a completely new 'truth' that could only be conveyed in abstract forms."[18]

Kandinsky was familiar with Steiner's writing, which he quoted in *Concerning the Spiritual in Art*, as well as in his teaching. "During his sojourn in Berlin 1907/8 he also attended Steiner's so-called *Architektenhausvorträge* [Architect House presentations]," wrote Sixten Ringbom in a penetrating study of Kandinsky's art.[19] From Ringbom we also learn of Emy Dresler, who in 1908 met Rudolf Steiner, joined the Theosophical Society, and was responsible for the stage decorations of Steiner's Mystery Dramas in Munich in 1910-13, and then continued as a collaborator in the work at Dornach. It was Emy Dresler who obtained a copy of Steiner's lecture cycle *The East in the Light of the West* for Kandinsky.[20] The more Kandinsky read Steiner's vivid accounts of his suprasensible experiences, often first published as articles in the journal *Luzifer-Gnosis*,[21] the greater became the impact of these teachings, "not only for [Kandinsky's] theories but even more for his paintings. For what Steiner describes as inner experiences resulting from imaginative knowledge is in fact literally echoed by Kandinsky in his art."[22] Another writer describes how Kandinsky in his *Composition IV* "painted something like a schematic image of the theosophical path leading to the attainment of knowledge of higher worlds. In no other of Kandinsky's works is the relationship of Steiner's epistemology so close and so complex as in this composition."[23] Throughout his life Kandinsky's paintings moved more and more toward the purely abstract, a progress inseparably linked with his deeply spiritual views.

From 1914 to 1921, Kandinsky was in Moscow, then returned to Germany. The next year he become a teacher at the Bauhaus, the design school founded in 1919 in Weimar. It was not until 1930 that the Bauhaus concentrated on architecture—under the direction of Mies van der Rohe, generating a strict, rigid architectural style that is now thought of as the school's chief contribution. But under the direction of Walter Gropius (an architect who was determined the school should reflect the unity of all the arts) and with the active participation of Kandinsky and others, for three years the school espoused Expressionism. "The primal image of the Bauhaus, which appeared on the front of Gropius's four-page prospectus of 1919 … was Lyonel Feininger's angular black-and-white woodcut of a crystalline church … This imaginary structure, as much lighthouse as sanctuary, was intended to evoke not specifically religious sentiments but rather the uplifting and unifying spirit of the great cathedral-building enterprises of the Middle Ages."[24]

Expressionism

For all Steiner's uniqueness, today his architecture is regularly discussed in general and architectural reference works under one or other of two different styles, "Organic" or "Expressionist." The meaning of the term "Expressionism" evolved over the period 1905-1930. In early use it was applied to any art that displayed a strong emotion, that emphasized personal vision rather than observation and knowledge. For a time it was used to denote all new or revolutionary art movements.

Expressionism spread through the world of art, particularly in Europe, and not just in painting. Franz Kafka attended Rudolf Steiner's lectures in Prague and found them "very stimulating."[25] Robert Wiene's 1920 film *The Cabinet of Dr. Caligari* and F. W. Murnau's 1922 *Nosferatu*, among a number of others, adapted many of the images and approaches of German Expressionist art to thrill audiences.

Eventually the word Expressionism came to be applied more specifically to "the primitivizing Bridge group (*Die Brücke*) … and the more abstract and intellectually oriented Blue Rider group (*Der Blaue Reiter*) in Munich, whose leader was the Russian Wassily Kandinsky."[26] Andrew Beard linked Steiner's architecture with "the idea of Gesamtkunstwerk (total work of art), of which Richard Wagner, for example, was an exponent."[27]

Beard associated the design of the two Goetheanum buildings with the work of well-known Expressionist architects—Antonio Gaudi, Saint Elia, Herman Finsterlin, Hans Scharoun, Eero Saarinen, and Erich Mendelsohn.[28] Mendelsohn was the only other architect beside Steiner who managed to design an Expressionist building in concrete[29]: the Einstein Tower in Potsdam of 1919-21. The webs connecting artists and architects of those days also connected Mendelsohn with the Expressionist groups *Die Brücke* and *Der Blaue Reiter* and later with the group that staged the Exhibition for Unknown Architects in Berlin, for which Gropius wrote the introductory leaflet in April 1919.

Sam Hunter and John Jacobus see the first Goetheanum as "a distant cousin of the architecture of Otto Wagner and the Viennese Secession. In contrast, the second building is a more extravagantly sculpted work rivaling Gaudi, so unusual in shape as to defy description in familiar architectural terms." They consider it "the one challenging realization of the notion of the Cathedral of the Future referred to in Expressionist literature, though … its opacity is a world removed from most Expressionist projects."[30]

Steiner continued to expand his own views on art. "It is possible to liberate color from context," he said. "If for example the juxtaposition of one color with another is one that is never found in nature … one must feel in actual experience that what comes to expression there does so through its own inherent impulse."[31] And in 1918 he commented directly on the art movement Expressionism: "What we offer is truly a work of art only when the legitimate effort toward visions enables us to successfully guess which pictorial or sculptural form we must offer the soul to counterbalance its visionary urge. It seems that many modern perspectives generally labeled 'Expressionism' come close to this truth, and their explanations come close to discovering what I have just said; but they do not go far enough."[32]

Organicism

"'[O]rganic architecture' in the twentieth century became the name of particular styles of building, such as those of Frank Lloyd Wright, Alvar Aalto or Rudolf Steiner," Caroline van Eck wrote in her expanded thesis on organicism in nineteenth century architecture.[33] "They are clearly distinguished by a marked use of materials, handling of space, approach to design and by their own ideologies." Another to claim Steiner as a creator of organic architecture is Reinhold Fäth. "One of Steiner's principles of organic design is that, within a building, 'nothing is there for its own sake alone,'" he writes. "Steiner related the design of the Goetheanum to the concept of metamorphosis, which he had found in Goethe's writings on the formation and transmutation of organic forms, as described in *Die Metamorphose der Pflanzen* [*The Metamorphosis of Plants*], and used the capitals on the columns in the first Goetheanum as examples to explain how the principle of metamorphosis may be applied … 'When we project the specific organization of the human body into the space outside it, then we have architecture.'"[34]

Steiner's architecture exhibits some parallels with that of the great Chicago architect Louis Sullivan, and it was a direct influence on Frank Lloyd Wright. Van Eck cites what Wright himself had to say: "What we call organic architecture is no mere aesthetic cult nor fashion but an actual movement based upon a profound idea of a new integrity of human life wherein art, science, religion are one: Form and Function seen as One, of such is Democracy."[35] In his early career Wright was employed by Sullivan, who shortly became Wright's mentor. Sullivan believed that the forms found in nature had evolved to meet the demands of their environment, that they were designed to perform particular functions, and thought that buildings should be designed on the same basis ("form ever follows function," he famously said).[36] From this it was a short step for Sullivan to declare his architecture organic, and, in the book revealing his theory of architecture, to call it a new faith. He declared: "… architecture in its material nature and in its animating essence is a plastic art … with its unceasing faith in man as free spirit! as creator, possessed of a physical sense indistinguishable from the spiritual, and of innate plastic powers whose fecundity and beneficence surpass our present scope of imagination."[37] This was the rich formulation of ideas, beliefs, and principles in which Wright developed his own architecture, and it was Sullivan's faith that prepared Wright for what eventually deepened his own architecture. "Wright insisted that his buildings be organic—that is, unified in conception from the largest principle to the smallest detail … [H]e was indeed the last surviving practitioner of ideas fostered by … the Arts and Crafts Movement, the Aesthetic Movement, and the various schools of Art Nouveau. Those ideas included … the quest for the fully integrated work of art, or *Gesamtkunstwerk* … Moreover … the architect's huge debt to Ralph Waldo Emerson—particularly Emerson's view of nature as the countenance of the divine—puts Wright firmly among the

Transcendentalists …"[38] Like Steiner and Kandinsky, Wright was also seeking "the spiritual in art."

Steiner's Influence on Later Architects

It was at about this time that George Gurdjieff, seeking a foundation for his own esoteric development, found the doctrine of theosophy.[39] Frank Lloyd Wright had fallen in love with Olga Ivanova Hinzenberg (known as Olgivanna), an adherent of Gurdjieff's, and it was she who brought Gurdjieff and theosophy to Wright. Initially at least, her attachment to Wright looks to have been part of Gurdjieff's plan to find a center in North America from which he could expand his movement, "The Work," as they knew that Wright was planning to vacate his premises. Some years later, when Solomon Guggenheim, the mining entrepreneur, decided to build a museum for his art collection, his art advisor Hilla Rebay suggested that Wright should be the architect. Rebay, an artist herself, had heard lectures by Rudolf Steiner early in the twentieth century, saw Wassily Kandinsky as one of the greatest artists of the time, and in 1930 visited Kandinsky's studio in Germany with Guggenheim. By 1943 Guggenheim was ready to build, Hilla Rebay was ready to direct Wright's work along theosophical lines, and Olgivanna, by then Wright's wife, was ready to add her own contribution from long reading of theosophy and Steiner.[40] The Solomon R. Guggenheim Museum, which was to be a "temple of the spirit," opened in New York City in 1959. Perhaps not coincidentally, its permanent collection holds one of the largest collections in the world— around 250 paintings—of Wassily Kandinsky's work.[41]

The presence of Rudolf Steiner in the artistic, architectural, and broad cultural world has been pervasive and persistent. The German architect Hans Scharoun, whose Berlin Philharmonic is a masterpiece of the post-1945 era, started to pursue the idea of organic buildings at about the same time as Steiner, whom he admired openly. Avoiding symbolism and elements of mythology, Scharoun's architecture "attempted to develop the artistic forms of [his] designs directly out of the 'essence of the building task'," Peter van der Ree wrote. He went on to say that "a building should function like the 'organ' of a living creature," noting that Scharoun's designs for schools "seem to have had a considerable influence on the Steiner schools that were built in the 1970s and '80s." Van der Ree added that "Scharoun's understanding of the school as a social organism … has been realized in many Steiner schools."[42] Other architects whose work reflected the impression made on them by Steiner's buildings included Richard Neutra and Le Corbusier. The Catalan architect Antoni Gaudi is often mentioned as the creator of an organic style, though only a little of it, impressive though it is, can be likened to Steiner's. The most striking, and certainly the best known, of Gaudi's buildings is the magnificent, still unfinished cathedral Sagrada Familia, which deliberately evokes the natural growth of plants and trees. Two buildings that are less distant from Steiner's architectural approach are Casa Milá and Casa Batlló, large houses he designed for wealthy families in Barcelona.

The Spiritualization of Built Form

Steiner's contribution to architectural style, in the mind of at least one writer on architecture, should more properly be identified as the spiritualization of built form. "His work," Ákos Moravánszky wrote, "was certainly influenced by what could be called the theory of empathy." According to this view, the basis of the psychological empathy with the structural system is gravity. When one looks at a building as it stands on its site, on the ground, one's first and fundamental reaction is to ask what holds it up, a reaction one would not have in looking at a bird, say, or a cloud, or a lake. Expounding Steiner's views, Moravánszky added that the Greek temple was based on a purely physical understanding of space and gravity. He cited Steiner's conclusion: "But the spirit is not a mere mechanist and dynamist; it reveals itself not only in the relations of space and power—the spirit is alive and consequentially it gives the building a living expression."[43]

In the morning of January 1, 1923, while the ruins of the first Goetheanum still smoldered, Steiner determined to rebuild, though the destruction of his creation surely hastened his death. While the design of the original building was his, his contribution to the second was considerably less. In 1924, he determined that the new building would be in concrete. Using plastiline (a material made of clay powder mixed with oil and wax instead of the water used in Plasticine) he created a model as the basis for its design. "The model assumed particular importance as Steiner was unable to participate further in the design process: he died after a long illness in March 1925."[44]

The second Goetheanum has been variously called the successor to the first, its memorial, the product of mourning, and "a document of the movement's development since the time of its foundation." To some anthroposophists in its early days it seemed a lesser building, perhaps in part because the decision to use concrete meant that it could not be put together in the same painstaking, hand-crafted way the first had been. Marie Steiner, Steiner's wife, called the new building "this simpler spiritual home." Steiner himself considered it but a pale shadow of the first.

Later judgments have differed. The architect Hans Scharoun declared the second Goetheanum "the most important building of the first half of the 20th century." The architectural historian Wolfgang Pehnt went further, calling it "one of the most magnificent pieces of sculptural architecture of the twentieth century."[45]

It is no longer possible to make a comparison of the two magnificent buildings Rudolf Steiner designed in that Swiss village of two thousand people. He says in this lecture that he meant for the building to nurture the work of anthroposophy, "calling forth the faculties that slumber within each human soul … actually rising up into the realm where suprasensory forces and beings reveal their existence to us … to the world of the senses, and this is revealed within our building." One can go and see Steiner's second major approach to nurturing anthroposophy, but not the first. May this book help the reader to understand how Steiner's first Goetheanum also achieved this object.

---

1. Wolfgang Pehnt, Expressionist Architecture (Stuttgart: Verlag Gerd Hatje, 1973; English translation, London: Thames and Hudson, 1973), 137-8. For a general overview of the secondary literature on the first Goetheanum, see the appended "Bibliographic Essay" by Frederick Amrine.

2. Steiner's lecture in Berlin of July 3, 1918.

3. Hella Wiesberger, in Rudolf Steiner's Collected Works (CW) 285; *Rosicrucianism Renewed: The Unity of Art, Science, and Religion: The Theosophical Congress of Whitsun 1907*, trans. Marsha Post (Great Barrington, MA: SteinerBooks, 2007); see Frederick Amrine's appended bibliographic essay for further discussion.

4. Ulrich Conrads, ed., *Programs and Manifestoes on 20th-century Architecture* (Cambridge, MA: Massachusetts Institute of Technology, 1970).

5. Bruno Taut, *The City Crown*, translated by Ulrike Altenmüller-Lewis and Matthew Mindrup (Burlington, VT: Ashgate, 2015).

6. Two other volumes of Steiner's lectures on architecture and the first Goetheanum, volumes 287 and 288 of Steiner's Complete Works, are forthcoming (2017) from SteinerBooks.

7. Pehnt, op. cit., 34.

8. Steiner's extensive fundamental concepts for the Goetheanum were rendered into plans, elevations, cross-sections, details, and working drawings by the architect Carl Schmid-Curtius, who worked on the project in the early years until he had a falling-out with Steiner; for the final

stages of construction the architects were Ernst Aisenpreis, Hermann Ratzenberger, Hermann Moser, and Albert von Baravalle.

9. Pehnt, 137-39.

10. Rudolf Steiner, *The Riddle of Humanity*, lecture of July 29, 1916 (London: Rudolf Steiner Press, 1990), 1-2.

11. See especially CW 288.

12. Rudolf Steiner, *Architecture as a Synthesis of the Arts* (CW 286), lecture of June 17, 1914, (London: Rudolf Steiner Press, 1990).

13. Steiner's own Mystery Dramas (1910-1913). See CW 14: Rudolf Steiner, *Four Mystery Dramas*, trans. Ruth and Hans Pusch (Great Barrington, MA: SteinerBooks, 2014).

14. Rudolf Steiner, *Art as Spiritual Activity*, edited and introduced by Michael Howard (Hudson, NY: Anthroposophic Press, 1998), p. 94.

15. Thomas Steinfeld, "Modernism's Occult Roots," *Axess Magasin* (Stockholm), July 1, 2010.

16. Herbert Kühn, "Expressionismus und Sozialismus" in *Neue Blätter für Kunst und Dichtung*, II (1919-20), no. 2, 29.

17. Peter Fingesten, "Spirituality, Mysticism and Non-objective Art," *The Art Journal*, XXI:1. Fall 1961, 2-6.

18. Steinfeld, op. cit.

19. Sixten Ringbom, *The Sounding Cosmos: A Study in the Spiritualism of Kandinsky and the Genesis of Abstract Painting* (Turku, Finland: Abo Akademi, 1970), 37.

20. ibid., 64.

21. See, for instance, *Wie erlangt man Erkenntnisse der höheren Welten?*, first published as articles in *Luzifer-Gnosis*, 13-28, Berlin 1904-1905; available in English as *How to Know Higher Worlds* (Hudson, NY: Anthroposophic Press, 1994).

22. Ringbom, op. cit., 136.

23. Hubertus Gassner, "Abstraction as Redemption—Kandinsky and Theosophy," in Walter Kugler and Simon Baur, editors, *Rudolf Steiner in Art and Architecture* (Cologne, 2007), quoted in Walter Kugler, "'World Spirit, Where are You?!': Rudolf Steiner and the Emergence of the Modern Age," *Rudolf Steiner: Alchemy of the Everyday*, catalogue of Vitra Design Museum exhibition, Weil am Rhein, Germany, September 2011 to March 2012, 33.

24. Martin Filler, *Makers of Modern Architecture* [Vol. 2] (New York: New York Review of Books, 2013), 48-52.

25. Steinfeld, op. cit.

26. Sam Hunter and John Jacobus, *Modern Art: from post-impressionism to the present; painting - sculpture - architecture* (New York: Abrams, 1976), 95.

27. For further discussion of the concept, see the bibliographic essay in the appendix of this volume.

28. Steiner, *Architecture: an Introductory Reader*, compiled by Andrew Beard (Forest Row: Sophia Books, 2003), 2.

29. Or apparently so. Because of the cost and difficulties of framing and a shortage of materials, in reality the building was built in brick with a stucco facing.

30. Hunter and Jacobus, op. cit., 192.

31. Steiner's lecture in Dornach of October 10, 1914.

32. Steiner's lecture in Munich of February 15, 1918.

33. Caroline van Eck, *Organicism in nineteenth-century architecture: an inquiry into its theoretical and philosophical background* (Amsterdam: Architectura & Natura Press: 1994), 258. While dismissing Steiner's work off-handedly, Van Eck is eager to say that it does not lie within the genre of nineteenth century organicism that is her subject.

34. Steiner's lecture in Dornach of December 29, 1914, in Reinhold J. Fäth, "Goetheanum style and aesthetic individualism," *Rudolf Steiner: Alchemy of the Everyday*, op. cit., 138.

35. Wright, *An Organic Architecture: The Architecture of Democracy* (1939), 47, in Van Eck, op. cit., 266.

36. Louis Sullivan, *A System of Architectural Ornament According with a Philosophy of Man's Powers* (1923).

37. Louis Sullivan, *The Autobiography of an Idea* (Press of the American Institute of Architects, 1924), 328

38. Martin Filler, *Makers of Modern Architecture* [Vol. 1] (New York: New York Review of Books, 2007), 20.

39. James Webb, *The Harmonious Circle: the lives and work of G. I. Gurdjieff, P. D. Ouspensky, and their followers* (New York: G. P. Putnam's Sons, 1980).

40. Roger Friedland and Harold Zellman, *The Fellowship: The Untold Story of Frank Lloyd Wright & the Taliesin Fellowship* (Regan, 2006), 50-378 passim.

41. Filler, Vol. 2, op. cit. (2013), 56.

42. Peter van der Ree, "Living thought and plastic art: Rudolf Steiner and organic architecture," *Rudolf Steiner: Alchemy of the Everyday*, op. cit., 189.

43. Steiner, *Wege zu einem neuen Baustil* (Dornach: Rudolf Steiner Verlag, 1992) 146, quoted in Ákos Moravánszky, "The Rudolf Steiner Goetheanum," *Domus* (Milan), 15 February 2011.

44. Moravánszky, 2011, ibid.

45. Pehnt, op. cit., 148.

Goethe and Goetheanism

FROM *DAS GOETHEANUM*, MARCH 25, 1923[1]

Anyone who contemplated the separate forms that had conjoined themselves in a living articulation to compose the overall *gestalt* of the Goetheanum could see how Goethe's ideas regarding metamorphosis had entered right into the building. These ideas came to Goethe when he attempted to comprehend the variety of the vegetal kingdom as a spiritual unity. In order to attain that goal, he sought the archetypal plant.[2] He conceived it as an ideal *gestalt* underlying all plants. Within that *gestalt*, one organ could develop itself to a high level of size and perfection, while others remained small and nondescript. In this way, it was possible to think up an endless number of specialized forms that would flow from the ideal archetype; and then one could allow one's glance to roam over the outer forms of the whole vegetal kingdom. In the one form it was possible to see this aspect, and, in another, that aspect of the conceptual image derived from the archetypal plant had been realized. The whole world of plants was *one single* plant, manifesting itself in the most various forms.

---

1. This short essay by Rudolf Steiner was originally published in the periodical *Das Goetheanum* on March 25, 1923. All references are to the building which has come to be called the "first Goetheanum," which was largely of wood, and not the "second Goetheanum," sculpted in concrete, that stands on the same site today.

2. *Urpflanze.* See especially Goethe's botanical treatise of 1790. The English-language edition of choice is now Johann Wolfgang von Goethe, *The Metamorphosis of Plants* (Cambridge, MA: MIT Press, 2009), trans. Douglas Miller, with an introduction and beautiful color photographs of the species Goethe describes by Gordon L. Miller. The German-language edition published by Verlag Freies Geistesleben (Stuttgart 1960) features Steiner's commentary plus excellent black-and-white engravings. The secondary literature on Goethe's scientific writings is vast, but the following three studies in English can be recommended as introductions: *Goethe and the Sciences: A Reappraisal*, ed. Frederick Amrine and Francis J. Zucker, Boston Studies in the Philosophy of Science 97 (Dordrecht: Reidel, 1987); Henri Bortoft, *The Wholeness of Nature: Goethe's Way Toward a Science of Conscious Participation in Nature* (Hudson, NY: Lindisfarne Press, 1996); and *Goethe's Way of Science: A Phenomenology of Nature*, ed. David Seamon and Arthur Zajonc, SUNY Series in Environmental and Architectural Phenomenology (Albany: SUNY Press, 1998).

What Goethe assumed in this process, however, is that a formative principle is at work within the variety of organisms, and that human beings emulate that principle through the inward mobility of their faculty of thinking. In doing so, he ascribed a capacity to human knowledge whereby it transcends the mere observation of outer beings and events in order to coalesce with them into a unity.

Goethe applied this same principle to our understanding of the individual plant as well. Within the leaf he saw the whole plant as already ideally present in the simplest way. And in the variegated forms of the plant he saw a leaf already formed in a complicated way. He saw the foliage of many different plants bound up into a unity again in accordance with the principle of the leaf. Likewise, the various forms in the anatomy of animals were for him transformations of a single underlying organ; and in the animal kingdom as a whole he saw manifold projections of an ideal "archetypal animal."[3]

Goethe did not work out this idea comprehensively, however. Conscientiousness led him to stop short halfway—especially with regard to the animal kingdom. He did not permit mere thoughts to proceed so far that the forms he had elaborated conceptually were no longer confirmed by the empirical facts.

Two different stances are possible vis-à-vis this Goethean idea of metamorphosis. You can consider it an interesting aspect of Goethe's peculiar way of thinking and let it go at that.

Or you can try to begin thinking in a Goethean way. Then what happens is that mysteries of nature do indeed reveal themselves to you, in ways that otherwise remain inaccessible.

When I realized this more than forty years ago, I wrote in my introductions to the Kürschner edition of his scientific works that Goethe was the Copernicus and the Kepler of the lifeworld.[4] My assumption was that, with regard to the lifeless world of inorganic phenomena, the "Copernican revolution" was the discovery that some things are independent of the human

---

3. For a selection of Goethe's writings on zoology, see Johann Wolfgang von Goethe, *Scientific Studies*, vol. 12 of the Suhrkamp Edition [in English], ed. and trans. Douglas Miller (New York: Suhrkamp Publishers, 1988), pp. 111-128. Goethe's ideas on zoology have since been elaborated more fully by many others, notably by Wolfgang Schad in his classic study *Man and Mammals* (Garden City, NY: Waldorf Press, 1977).

4. The introductions to the various sections of the so-called Kürschner edition were later published as vol. 1 of Steiner's Collected Works. The latest English edition is a handsome offering from the Anthroposophic Press, *Nature's Open Secret: Rudolf Steiner's Introductions to Goethe's Scientific Works* (2000). See also Steiner's philosophical monograph *Goethe's Theory of Knowledge: An Outline of the Epistemology of His Worldview,* (Great Barrington, MA: SteinerBooks, 2008).

observer. Goethe's Copernican revolution was his discovery of the very different kind of human spiritual activity that is required to understand the organic world's living mobility.

Goethe brought about *his own* "Copernican revolution" by importing the kind of spiritual activity in which he had engaged as an artist into the conduct of science. He sought the path from artist to scientist, and he found it. That is why the anthropologist Heinroth[5] called Goethe's scientific thinking "objective."[6] Goethe declared himself profoundly satisfied with that characterization. He adopted the word, and termed his literary work "objective" as well. In that way, he revealed how closely artistic and scientific activity were allied in his soul.

Entering sympathetically into Goethe's way of thinking gave us the courage to bring Goethe's view of metamorphosis back into the arts again. That contributed importantly to the architectural theory underlying the Goetheanum. Within the lifeworld, nature creates in forms that grow out of each other. We can approach this creativity of nature herself if we shape our own artistic forming sculpturally by comprehending lovingly and empathetically how nature lives within metamorphoses.

A building can genuinely be called "Goetheanum" if it has made a bold attempt to realize its architectural and sculptural forms by entering empathetically into Goethe's view of metamorphosis.

By the time the Goetheanum was begun, colleagues who were rigorously trained in the most varied fields had already found their way to anthroposophy. Since there was every prospect of their going on to apply anthroposophical methods within the various individual disciplines, I felt justified in suggesting that we add a further title to our building: School of Spiritual Science.[7]

---

5. Johann C. F. A. Heinroth [1773-1843], a professor in Leipzig who "spoke favorably" of Goethe's scientific work in his *Manual of Anthropology* (1822).

6. *gegenständlich*. This German word might also be translated "concrete." See Goethe's brief essay "Significant Help Given by an Ingenious Turn of Phrase" in his *Scientific Studies*, pp. 39-41.

7. Wilhelm Dilthey (1833-1911) had used the same term (usually in the plural, *Geisteswissenschaften*) to distinguish the "humanities" (as we call them in English today) from natural science (*Naturwissenschaft*), argueing that the latter seeks to explain in terms of cause and effect, whereas the former explains by relating parts to wholes. (See W. Dilthey, *Introduction to the Human Sciences*, Selected Works, vol. 1 [Princeton: Princeton University Press, 1991]). But a century earlier, Hegel had described a "science of the spirit" (*Wissenschaft des Geistes*), and already during his theosophical phase, Steiner employs the word *Geisteswissenschaft* in a fundamentally different sense that makes it a synonym for "anthroposophy." In such contexts, the term is best translated by the firmly established locution "spiritual science." The School of Spiritual Science continues to this day, and it is still housed in a building called the Goetheanum.

For almost ten years, friends of anthroposophy have worked on this building. Costly sacrifices of a material kind were made on many sides: artists, architects, and scientists collaborated with the greatest devotion. Everyone within the circle of anthroposophy who could work on the building did so.[8] The most difficult tasks were shouldered willingly. The spirit of the anthroposophical worldview worked upon this "Goetheanum" with heartfelt enthusiasm. The great majority of the construction workers, who were initially indifferent at best, had decided by 1922 that the misapprehensions about anthroposophy that had become so widespread were unfounded.

My own thoughts and those of my colleagues were focused on the continuation of our work. We had announced a scientific course for the end of December and the beginning of January. Friends of the anthroposophical cause from many lands were present again.

Years ago we added to the other ongoing artistic activity eurythmy and recitation,[9] directed by Frau Marie Steiner,[10] who has made this one of her many tasks. On New Year's Eve there was a performance of eurythmy from 5-7 p.m. At 8 p.m. I began my lecture, which ended at 9:30. I had spoken in an anthroposophical way about the connection between human beings and the phenomena of the annual rhythms. A short time after that, the Goetheanum stood in flames, and by the morning of New Year's Day, 1923, it had burned down to the concrete foundation.

---

8. World War I had made it impossible for many members to travel to Dornach.

9. Beginning in 1912, Rudolf Steiner began to convey a new art of movement that he called "eurythmy." In his first, brief talk on the subject (August 28, 1913), Steiner described it as "the play of movement which stands in a certain harmony with the movements that express cosmic tones and cosmic words." Right from the beginning, he imagined that it would have three different aspects: artistic, pedagogical, and curative. All three aspects are fully developed today. See CW 277a, *Eurythmy: Its Birth and Development*, trans. Alan Stott (Anastasi, 2002); CW 278, originally translated under the title *Eurythmy as Visible Music* (London: Rudolf Steiner Press, 1977) but more recently by Alan Stott under the title *Eurythmy as Visible Singing*, 2 vols., 4th edn. (Stourbridge: The Anderida Music Trust, 2013); and CW 279, *Eurythmy as Visible Speech* (London: Rudolf Steiner Press, 1984). Steiner developed eurythmy in part as a dramatic technique for depicting spiritual action in the stagings of Goethe's *Faust* and his own Mystery Dramas that he directed; for texts relating to that aspect, see CW 277c, *The Early History of Eurythmy* (Great Barrington, MA: SteinerBooks, 2015). In collaboration with his wife Marie, Steiner also developed a new art of recitation that is also called in English "creative speech." The main sources here are CW 281, *Poetry and the Art of Speech*, (London School of Speech Formation, 1981) and CW 282, *Speech and Drama*, (Spring Valley, NY: Anthroposophic Press, 1960). CW 281, which includes an outstanding selection of English poems illustrating Steiner's points, is unfortunately a rare book that cries out to be reprinted.

10. Née Marie von Sivers (1867-1948), Rudolf Steiner's second wife, who collaborated closely with him on artistic impulses during his lifetime.

The Architectural Idea of the First Goetheanum

BERN, JUNE 29, 1921

ANTHROPOSOPHY HAS FOUND a new center for its outer activity in Dornach near Basel. The creation of this new center of activity, which is called the Goetheanum, School for Spiritual Science, arose naturally out of the spreading of anthroposophy. After anthroposophy had been set forth over a period of many years by me and others in the most various places, initially in a conceptual form, by way of lectures and such, around the year 1909 or 1910 many began to feel a need for means other than mere thoughts and mere words to reveal and communicate to the souls of our contemporaries the intentions of anthroposophy.

And so it came about that a series of Mystery Dramas that I had written were performed, initially in Munich.[1] These dramas attempted to depict in imaginative, dramatic form the things which anthroposophy must speak if it's to be true to its whole inner nature. The entire process of education within the civilized world over the last three to four centuries has accustomed us to seek knowledge principally through external sensory observation and through the application of the human intellect to this external sensory observation. All of our modern sciences, to the extent that they're still viable at all, have essentially arisen through the interaction between empirical data and their intellectual elaboration. The historical disciplines as they're practiced today have developed in essentially the same way.

It's intellectuality above all that the modern world trusts when it comes to

---

1. Rudolf Steiner wrote and directed four Mystery Dramas: *The Portal of Initiation* (1910), *The Soul's Probation* (1911), *The Guardian of the Threshold* (1912) and *The Souls' Awakening* (1913). See CW 14, Rudolf Steiner, *Four Mystery Dramas*, trans. Ruth and Hans Pusch (Great Barrington, MA: SteinerBooks, 2014). All four were performed originally in Munich, which had become the center of the artistic avant-garde in Central Europe, and they are in many ways typically Expressionist. Kandinsky and Schönberg among many others experienced the Mystery Dramas and were influenced by them during these last years leading up to World War I.

cognition. It's intellectuality to which we've become ever more accustomed. And so it is, of course, that we've come to believe more and more that everything presented to the world as the results of research can be communicated entirely in intellectual terms. Indeed, there are epistemological treatises and other such academic writings which seemingly prove that something can be valid in the eyes of our contemporaries only if it can be justified intellectually. What can't be clothed in intellectual terms isn't considered valid cognition. Anthroposophy refuses to call a halt where modern science rightly sets limits to its own kind of knowledge.[2] Anthroposophy strives to transcend those limits to knowledge, and thereby anthroposophy came to realize ever more deeply and clearly that the intellectual mode couldn't be the only valid form of communication. They can go on and on demonstrating with all kinds of specious reasons that all cognition must be couched in an intellectual form if it's to satisfy humanity; they can go on and on demonstrating this with specious reasons. But if the world is constructed in a way that can't be expressed merely in concepts and ideas; if it really is the case for example—especially if we want to come to know the laws of human evolution—that those laws need to be expressed in pictorial form, then we really have to attempt something other than depicting the world using words in theoretical lectures. We need to evolve modes of depiction other than the merely intellectual.

And so it was that I felt the need to express something which is completely alive, especially within the evolution of humanity, not merely in theoretical terms, by means of words, but also by way of dramatic depictions. That's what gave rise to my four Mystery Dramas, which were performed initially in a conventional theater. That was, shall we say, the first step towards an expanded presentation of the insights that anthroposophy intends to reveal, something that arose out of anthroposophy itself.

Let me assure you, it wasn't my own idea: in the course of developments that led gradually to the need for an external dramatic presentation, the thought

---

2. *naturwissenschaftliche Erkenntnisgrenze*. Steiner grappled with such epistemological questions in his early philosophical writings, especially in his "basic book" CW 4, *The Philosophy of Freedom: The Basis for a Modern World Conception: Some results of introspective observation following the methods of Natural Science*, trans. Michael Wilson (London: Rudolf Steiner Press, 1964). (Alternative English translations are available under the titles *The Philosophy of Spiritual Activity* and *Intuitive Thinking as a Spiritual Path*.) "Limits to knowledge" is a reference to the mistaken neo-Kantian interpretation of the great German idealist that was pervasive in the late nineteenth century. For a systematic treatment of this topic within Steiner's later work, see CW 322, *The Boundaries of Natural Science*, tr. Frederick Amrine and Konrad Oberhuber, foreword Saul Bellow (Hudson, NY: Anthroposophic Press, 1983).

arose among certain friends of our cause that the activity of anthroposophy needed its own home. And after various attempts here and there to found such a home, we arrived at last on the hill in Dornach in the vicinity of Basel. Our friend Dr. Grosheintz donated a tract of land for this purpose, and we were able to erect upon the hill in Dornach this School of Spiritual Science, which we now call the "Goetheanum." The Goetheanum is also intended to become a home for the other arts that shall reveal anthroposophy to the world.

Now if just any old organization with this or that program had undertaken to create such a framework, such a house, under similar circumstances, what kind of architecture would they have chosen? They'd have turned to this or that architect, who perhaps wouldn't have bothered very much to feel or to sense or to come to know the content of anthroposophy; she simply would have executed the building in Classical or Gothic or Renaissance style, or in some other historical style. And then in such a building, which had grown out of completely different cultural presuppositions, we would have betrayed utterly the essence of anthroposophy in its many dimensions. That's how it could have gone in this regard and in regard to many other strivings within contemporary life, and doubtless that's what would have happened. But in the case of anthroposophy that couldn't be allowed to happen.

Last year we inaugurated our first series of courses on the various scientific disciplines in the School of Spiritual Science in Dornach.[3] What I said at that time was that anthroposophy didn't intend to bring to humanity merely science in the narrow sense; that anthroposophy didn't draw only from the accomplishments of empirical observation and the human intellect, but rather that it draws from wholeness, from our full human nature, and that it draws from the springs from which there flow religion on the one hand and art on the other.

The kind of art that anthroposophy intends to create shouldn't contain any abstract symbols or wooden allegories that merely shoehorn didacticism into external forms; no, that's in no way the case. Rather, what anthroposophy expresses in words can exert an effect through the word; it can form itself through the word. Anthroposophy can speak of spiritual events, of spiritual beings of the suprasensory world by having recourse to ideas and to the words that are their medium of expression. But the spiritual content that wills to reveal itself in this way is much too rich to be contained within words and

---

3. Published as CW 322, *The Boundaries of Natural Science* (see the previous note). The opening lecture on the great intellectual dilemmas of the age is especially eloquent.

ideas alone; it strives for form, for the image, metamorphoses itself all on its own into art, into genuine art, not into some kind of allegorical or symbolic language. That's not what we mean when we speak of "the art of Dornach."

When we speak of the art of Dornach, then what we are doing first and foremost is indicating the primal font from which human existence and cosmic existence well forth.[4] What we experience in this original source, if we gain access to it in the ways we have also described here so often—we can clothe that in words; we can clothe it in ideas. But we can also allow it to flow directly into artistic form without expressing ideas allegorically or symbolically.

What can live in the arts and also in religion (I could say more about this, but it's not necessary today) is a fully equivalent expression of something that can also be given in conceptual form. Thus, right from the beginning, anthroposophy has the potential to flow from springs that can also be the pure, primal sources of art and religion.[5] When we speak of religion in Dornach, when we speak about religious feelings, we're not talking about a science that has been made into a religion, but rather about something that is the origin of elemental religious power. And when we speak of art, we likewise mean an originary, elemental act of artistic creation.

So when many visitors to the Goetheanum, and especially folks who have not visited but heard stories about it, slander our building in Dornach and say that what one finds there is this or that allegorical, symbolic mode of depiction, then that's just what it is—a slander. There isn't a single symbol anywhere in the building in Dornach. Everything depicted there has flowed directly from artistic feeling into form. And it really is the case that I feel I'm offering a cheap substitute whenever people assume that I will explain the building in Dornach with words. To be sure, when lecturing outside of Dornach we can talk about the building in the way that we lecture for example on various episodes in the history of art. But when people are experiencing the building in Dornach directly, then I always feel that it's actually a kind of cheap substitute if I go on and try to explain the experience in words. An explanation of this kind is actually necessary only in the way that one needs to explain, shall we

_____

4. As should be clear from the larger context, what Steiner is advocating here is precisely the antithesis of any return *ad fontes*: not a recovery of authoritative traditions, but the discovery of new sources welling up from the unconscious. Steiner's aesthetics is archetypally modern in this sense.
5. Here Steiner invokes an image that is genuinely archetypal. (Indeed, Jung argues that water is the archetypal symbol of the unconscious as such.) Cf. also the central panel of Jan van Eyck's mystical *Ghent Altarpiece* of 1432, "The Adoration of the Lamb of God," in which a fountain symbolizes the welling forth of the Holy Spirit.

say, the *Sistine Madonna*: people need to learn the vocabulary of the worldview out of which our artistic forms have arisen, in the same way that Raphael's painting has emanated from the Christian worldview. In both cases, it's not that something is being symbolized, but rather that something of the nature of an idea has really lived as a feeling within the artist.

After he had written his poem *Ahasuerus in Rome*, the Austrian poet Hamerling was accused of having employed symbols.[6] Then he replied to his critics, saying rightly: what am I supposed to do, if I want to depict Nero in a vibrant and fully real way, in his real human nature, other than set him forth as the symbol of cruelty? After all, history itself has established Nero as the symbol of cruelty. The artist would deserve to be criticized not if his vivid depiction of Nero awakened within us the real symbol of cruelty, but rather if he placed before the audience some wooden allegory in place of a vibrant character. Even though the world that's depicted in Dornach is the suprasensible world, we've depicted a world that's been suprasensibly *viewed*, a suprasensible *reality*. It's not something that strives merely to transpose concepts symbolically or allegorically. That's the real reason why anthroposophy couldn't have been housed in just any old kind of building. Any pre-existing architectural style would have remained external to it, because anthroposophy isn't just a theory; in all its manifestations, anthroposophy is a living force, and it was fully capable of calling forth its own architectural style.

Of course, in retrospect we could trace a historical line of development, beginning with ancient architecture, which is characterized by displays of load-bearing and support. Then we could move on to the Gothic, where architecture transcends the dynamics of load-bearing and support, where the striving of the Gothic arch and cross vaulting are freed from the display of load-bearing and supporting; where a kind of transition to something living takes place.[7]

What we attempted in Dornach was to extend this living quality so far that the merely dynamic, metric, symmetrical qualities of earlier architectural styles have been metamorphosed into something that is truly organic. I know very well how much there is to criticize in this metamorphosis of geometrical,

---

6. Austrian poet, 1830-1889. Hamerling's talent was widely recognized in his own day, but today he is obscure. *Ahasuerus in Rome* (1866) is considered his best work.

7. No doubt Steiner is thinking principally here of Goethe's youthful essay "On German Architecture" of 1772, a panegyric to the Gothic cathedral in Strasbourg, France. Goethe describes the cathedral as "a living whole," raised up by the genius of its putative architect Erwin von Steinbach "like the mighty trees of God Himself."

metric, symmetrical forms into organic forms—forms that otherwise are to be found in the creations of nature—from the perspective of older architectural theories. But in no way have we sought to imitate any kind of organism naturalistically here. Rather, what we've tried to do is to enter empathetically into the organic, creative principle of nature herself. Just as you can enter empathetically into loading and supporting if you allow your columns to be topped with lintels; and just as you can also enter empathetically into the whole configuration of the Gothic style, in the striving depicted in its vaults and so on, it's also possible to enter empathetically into that inner formative dynamic, nature's formative processes, which are at work in the genesis of organic forms.

If we can enter into that genesis, then we arrive not at a naturalistic imitation of this or that superficial form, which can be found in the organic world, but rather we arrive at the ability to find surfaces that originate within the immediacy of the architectural experience. These surfaces then integrate themselves into the building as a whole in the same way that, let's say, the surface of an individual finger integrates itself into the whole of the human organism.

That's the essential experience that you can begin to have when confronting our building in Dornach—to the extent this initial attempt succeeded in accomplishing our ideal. What we were striving to do is something that can perhaps be experienced in this way: the smallest detail and the largest formal relationships, everything about the building has been conceived in such a way that each detail, located right where it is, is *thus* because it *must be so*. You only need to think about your own earlobes, for example.

The earlobe is a very small organ. But if you understand the organism as a whole, then you'll say to yourself: the earlobe couldn't be other than the way that it is; the earlobe can't be the little toe, it can't be the right thumb, but rather within the organism everything is in its place and everything in its place has taken a form that proceeds from the organism as a whole.

That's what we sought to do in Dornach. The whole building, everything about the architecture, has been conceived within the context of the whole. Every detail has been formed individually in the way that's dictated by its particular location. As I said, even though one can raise many objections, at least somebody *made an attempt* to develop from a merely geometrical-mechanical way of building to an architecture that builds with organic forms.[8] Of course

---

8. Steiner addresses the topic of organicism in architecture more extensively and systematically in a series of five lectures given in 1920-21. Together with Steiner's address at the dedication of the first Goetheanum (September 20, 1916), these lectures constitute CW 288, forthcoming from SteinerBooks.

someone could find similarities between this architectural style and other historical styles, but really one gets nowhere that way. And it's especially the creative artist who can't get anywhere in that way. Something like our building simply must arise out of elemental experience. That is why, when I am asked how the individual form was felt within the context of the whole, I can only answer as follows.

Take the nut as an example. Nuts have shells. This nutshell has been formed around the kernel in accordance with the same laws that gave rise to the kernel of the nut itself. We can't imagine this shell in any other way because the kernel is the way it is.

You're all familiar with anthroposophy. We speak about anthroposophy out of its own inner impulses. We clothe it in ideas. We comprehend it in the form of ideas. And so we live within the whole being of this anthroposophy—forgive me, it's a trivial comparison, but it's a comparison that makes clear how it is that one can only create a building such as ours in Dornach by working naïvely—we stand as it were within the kernel of the nut and within that kernel reside the same laws that need to be the source of the shell, the building that houses anthroposophy.

In the past I have often made another comparison. You see, in Austria there's a certain kind of cake that we call *Gugelhupf*.[9] I don't know whether it's called that here. And what I've said in the past is that we have to imagine that anthroposophy is the Bundt cake and the building in Dornach is the Bundt pan in which it's baked. The Bundt cake and its pan, they have to correspond completely with each other—and it's right if both correspond, which is to say if they stand in the same relationship to each other as the kernel and the shell of a nut.

But just because anthroposophy creates out of the fullness of human nature, it couldn't bear within it the discrepancy of taking just any old building and speaking into it. Anthroposophy is more than just a theory: it's life. That's why it had to provide not only the kernel, but also the shell, right down into the smallest details. Our building had to be created in keeping with the same inner lawfulness that informs all our speaking, that guides the performance of the Mystery Dramas, and out of which we are now performing eurythmy. Everything that we speak in words, that we see performed in eurythmy, that you will see performed in the Mystery Dramas, and in the other dramas that

---

9. The American variant on this Central European classic is the Bundt cake.

will be performed, has to resonate through the hall so that we see the walls with their forms and the paintings which are there clearly saying "yes" to it all. The eyes of the audience should receive these things as something in which they participate directly. Every column should speak in the same way that the mouth speaks when it's expressing anthroposophical truths. Just because it's simultaneously science, art, and religion, anthroposophy had to ignore all conventional architectural styles and devise instead its own architectural style. Now of course people can criticize this new style from top to bottom, but they forget that whatever emerges for the first time in evolution shows itself initially in an imperfect form. Let me assure you that I know about all the mistakes we've made, right down into the smallest details, and that I myself am the one who says: if I were to build this building a second time, I would build it in the same spirit, in keeping with the same laws, but most of its details and perhaps even the building as a whole would be entirely different. But when the time has come to take hold of an initiative, then we just have to take hold of it as best we can at that moment. By creating something in this way, one learns for the first time the actual laws of one's own nature. Such are the laws governing destiny within spiritual life; such are the laws of spiritual progress; and those laws were not violated when we constructed our building in Dornach.

So now our building rises up on the hill in Dornach. Our first task was to feel the main outlines of its forms, to feel how it raises itself up out of the hill in Dornach, right? That's why the ground floor was made of concrete. I sought to draw forth artistic forms from this unyielding material, and many people have sensed how these concrete forms join themselves to the rocky formations in the environment. Many have felt that in Dornach nature metamorphoses itself with a certain immediacy right into the forms of the buildings.

And then upon the horizontal terrace, on top of the first floor made of concrete, the wooden building rises up. This wooden building consists of two interlocking cylinders that are capped by two incomplete hemispheres. These two hemispheres intersect along their surface in such a way that the two hemispheres—two connected hemispheres—cap the cylindrical spaces by overlapping as it were. There's a larger space, the main hall; and there's a smaller space within which eurythmy is performed, Mystery Dramas are staged, and so forth. Between the two spaces is the speaker's podium. That's the main structure of the building.

And of course I shouldn't fail to mention that in recent years countless friends, especially people working in one or another academic discipline, have meanwhile perceived and acknowledged that the physical sciences, mathematics, history, medicine, law, sociology—that the most various disciplines can be fructified by anthroposophy. That is why we must go on to create in Dornach a true university, and our first concern has actually been to create something that's nothing other than a great auditorium for that purpose—of course also leaving open the possibility of communicating with the audience, with room for as many as a thousand people, in ways other than merely through the spoken word.

That our building has a kind of dualistic form in the way I just described, that it consists of two cylinders crowned by hemispheres, is the result of having felt clearly the tasks that anthroposophy must set itself, in light of the spirit of anthroposophy as it's pursued in Dornach. For the ultimate foundation is something that we call inner human development. Anthroposophy isn't something that can be attained merely by employing the usual, everyday faculty of judgment (although of course we presuppose and make use of that faculty everywhere). It can't be attained by using conventional methods of research, but only by calling forth the faculties that slumber within each human soul in the way I described in my book *How to Know Higher Worlds*,[10] only by actually rising up into the realm where suprasensory forces and beings reveal their existence to us. A suprasensory world reveals itself to the world of the senses, and this is revealed within our building. It's revealed when an audience of a thousand sits in the auditorium and from the other side they receive communications that provide knowledge of higher worlds—all of this, translated into artistic feeling, expresses itself directly in the forms of this building in Dornach with its double cupolas. Nothing there is meant to be symbolic in any sense. And thus I can also say: of course one could express this fundamental thought differently, but this was the artistic expression of the fundamental thought that came to me in a way that was necessary at that time.

And so it is that in the external form of the wooden building growing up out of the concrete—this wooden building which has a double cupola—coming up to the building from its surroundings, one sees in the configuration itself, in the forming of the surfaces, what it is that anthroposophy actually intends. That it really wasn't a matter of abstract concepts for us, but rather of real artistic feeling, is something that you can also see in our having procured Norwegian slate to cover both the cupolas. (We did this at a time when that

10. CW 10; *How to Know Higher Worlds* (Hudson, NY: Anthroposophic Press, 1994).

was still possible, before the War, but it still took a tremendous effort.) Once when I was on a lecture tour in 1913 between Christiania[11] and Bergen, I saw this wonderful Voss roofing slate.[12] And now this Norwegian slate glimmers on the double cupolas in the sunlight, so that you actually have the feeling: the greenish-grayish gleam that it reflects, that's something that belongs within this whole landscape—even though of course many people say that the landscape was desecrated by the building. Everyone can have his or her own point of view and everyone can be a critic. I never bother to counter criticism even if it's as foolish as this. It's only when people spread lies about Dornach and everything associated with it—something that's happening ever more frequently as time goes by—then to be sure, lies must be countered in the strongest terms. But I'll never object to criticism, no matter how foolish it may appear. So I let them go ahead and say that the building in Dornach has ruined the neighborhood. Maybe so. But to my mind, the care we took to see that even the reflection of the sun off the roof would be right for a landscape such as this shows how hard we tried to place something worthy in this location, which has indeed something extraordinary about it as a place.

And now I'll take the liberty of presenting a series of slides to show you what has arisen as this Goetheanum in Dornach. The slides should reveal to you in detail all the ways in which the architectural theory actually realized itself. By means of this architecture the same thing should present itself to the viewer pictorially that is communicated to the audience through the spoken word. What you see in Dornach should be the same thing that you hear in Dornach. Because it really was a renewal proceeding from the life of the spirit; because it represents a renewal of all the academic disciplines, there was a sense in which anthroposophy needed an entirely new kind of art.

---

11. Now Oslo
12. This extraordinary Norwegian slate takes its name from the location of the quarry near Vossevangen, east of Bergen. It is thought to be around 150 million years older than all other kinds of slate. Unusually high concentrations of quartzite and mica give it an exceptional shimmer.

SLIDE 1:   Here [pg. 17, opposite] you see the building—one of the cupolas is somewhat hidden here—and here the concrete foundation. This is the view that you get if you approach the building along a path that leads from the northwest to the west entrance. So here is the concrete foundation with the entrance; here is where you first enter. Further back inside this concrete structure are the coatrooms. After having used the coatrooms, you go up a set of stairs that takes you through this room on the right and left, up to the terrace. Then you go into the building via the main entrance and you arrive initially in an anteroom that leads into the main hall.[13]

You see here, from this terrace on up, the wooden building that's roofed with Nordic slate. The form over the west entrance is meant to be an organic form that grows out of the building as a whole. It's not something that can be found in the realm of organic nature and that has been imitated naturalistically; rather, what I sought to do was to penetrate into the process of organic creativity itself. I sought to give myself over to the process of organic formation within nature itself, so that it would be possible to create such organic forms anew. I sought to give the entire building a form that was organic, yet without violating any of the laws of structural dynamics. Let me say that again emphatically: without violating any dynamic or mechanical laws. Anyone who studies especially the inner architecture in Dornach will see that everywhere, even though the columns, piers, and so forth have been formed organically, it is an artifact of this very organic form that everything supports loads and all the loads are distributed properly without expressing any sense of supporting through the thickness of the columns or the weight of the materials. (The same principle was taken into consideration when shaping the external architecture, even though this was more difficult both for artistic reasons and also due to the nature of the construction process.) The right balance between load and support has also been addressed by way of organic forms, so that one has the feeling that the building itself senses loading and supporting simultaneously. One of our basic intentions for this building in working out of anthroposophical principles was that the building would express an appearance of consciousness, just as things actually are in the organic realm. And so in designing the building the attempt was made to move in the direction of organic form without sinning against the laws of mechanics, geometry, or symmetry.

---

13.   *Vorbau*. This element functions as a two-story westwork would in a Carolingian or Romanesque church.

SLIDE 2: Looking at the building from a bit farther away, and more from the west facade: here you see the concrete foundation, here the terrace, and then the main entrance. Here the same motif reveals itself again. The second cupola, the smaller one covering the stage, is hidden here; you see instead what joins it to the rest of the building as it were. At the point where the two cupolas join there are wings on the left and right. These contain dressing rooms for the performers in the Mystery Dramas or in presentations of eurythmy and so forth. They also contain some offices and such. So these are secondary structures here. In a moment we'll see the floor plan, which shows how these are integrated into the conception of the building as a whole.

SLIDE 3: Here you see the building from the southwest side: again the west entrance, the larger cupola, just a tiny bit of the smaller cupola, off to the south the southern wing; here you see the whole facade between west and south.

SLIDE 4: Here you see from the other side, from the north, the two spaces that are covered by cupolas, the main hall, one of the wings from the front, here the stage with its smaller cupola and the storage rooms, which are attached to the stage towards the east; and here is the terrace, under it the concrete foundation. That's the anteroom that leads to the west entrance.[14]

---

14. See the previous note in the discussion of Slide 1.

SLIDE 5: From somewhat farther away; here you're looking on from the northeast. These are the storage rooms. Here the smaller cupola between the two wings and here the Heating and Illumination Plant.

SLIDE 6:   And this is the remarkable building that's become so very controversial, the Heating and Illumination Plant. This is the view of the building when looking from the west side. Here the challenge was the need to work with concrete, which is a difficult material. And what I had to do as an artist here, working out of artistic laws and feelings, was to say to myself: so, given that we need to have machinery that will heat and light the building, let's think of that as the kernel and then ask, how should the nutshell be formed in such a way that it will provide the right basis for the chimney? If you'll pardon the hackneyed analogy, this principle of the nutshell has been carried out in detail here. And anyone who complains about such a building should consider what would've stood there otherwise, if we *hadn't* tried this experiment. The experiment might have turned out imperfectly, but otherwise a red brick chimney would be standing there! Basically, the right way to design a utility building is first of all to gain the necessary feel for the material with which you're working, and then to shape the outer form in a way that's thoroughly consonant with the function.

SLIDE 7 (*page 26*):   Here I've taken the liberty of showing you the entire floor plan. The main entry is from the west: you enter through various anterooms into the main hall. The main hall seats an audience of 900-1000. Here you see a gallery that's enclosed inwardly by seven columns on each side. There's only one line of symmetry: the west-east axis. That's the only axis of symmetry. The motifs of the building have been formed symmetrically only in relation to this axis of symmetry, the east-west axis; otherwise there are no repetitions. Hence the columns have been provided with capitals and bases that aren't the same, but rather are continually evolving. So we have a first column on the right and left, and a second column on the right and left, and to be sure the capitals and bases on the left are always the same as the corresponding capitals and bases on the right. But the column that follows always shows a different capital and base, and the motif of the architrave above it is also different. This feature is something that had emerged directly out of the organic architectural style; more specifically, it's an artistic expression of Goethe's theory of metamorphosis. Goethe worked out this theory of metamorphosis in a brilliant way, and I'm firmly convinced that it will play a major role in the future of the life sciences. Anyone who studies his deceptively simple little treatise *The Metamorphosis of Plants* published in 1790 recognizes it as a magnificent work of science—one that current scientific prejudices have denied sufficient appreciation. Briefly stated, Goethe sees the entire plant as a complicated leaf. He begins with the lowest leaf, the one closest to the ground; then he follows the leaves up to the buds, which are formed completely differently from the foliage leaves; then the blossom leaves, which are colored completely differently; and then on to the pistils and stamens, which display forms that are different yet again. Goethe wrote: everything that appears in such seemingly various forms in the leaves of the plants is such that it can be traced back to a single, ideal unity; it appears in different metamorphoses only to the outer senses. Essentially the leaf of the plant is always recapitulating the same basic form; that which is ever ideally the same is given various shapes, metamorphosed, only within sense perception. This metamorphosing constitutes the fundamental principle that underlies the shaping of everything living. And if we can also raise that up into artistic forming and shaping, then we can do the following.

We form the simplest capital or the simplest base for the first column that we have here, and then we immerse ourselves in the productive powers of nature. We begin by attempting to eavesdrop upon those productive powers—not with abstract thinking, but rather with inner feeling and the will to participate in nature's creating. Only then do we attempt to bring forth out of the simpler motif of the first column a somewhat more complicated motif in the second column—in the same way that a leaf standing higher up within the plant is more complicated than the leaf that preceded it, and yet is a metamorphosis of the lower leaf. So that actually all seven of these capitals have been called forth from each other; they have grown out of each other metamorphically like the vegetal forms that build upon each other in the growing plant. Hence, in these capitals, which don't merely repeat the same forms over and over, we see a genuine recreation of nature's own creation; from the first to the seventh, these capitals are caught up in a process of continual growth.

And so of course folks come along, see seven columns there—profoundly mystical! And yes, of course there are also members of the Anthroposophical Society who speak in all kinds of dark, mysterious allusions about the profound mysticism of these seven pillars and so forth. But there isn't anything behind them except artistic sensibility. When you arrive at the seventh column, then the motif of this seventh column stands in exactly the same relationship—if we really have created in the way that nature creates—as *dō* to *tï* in a musical scale, and just as the octave repeats *dō*, so we would have to repeat the first column if we proceeded to an eighth.

Here we see the boundary between the main hall and the stage, where the two cupolas join; right there stands the speaker's rostrum, which can be sunk into the floor because it needs to be removed whenever something is performed onstage. Here again are the twelve columns around the circumference, the boundary of the stage, the two wings for dressing rooms, and so on.[15]

---

15. See also Appendix 1: Addendum to the Discussion of Slide 7.

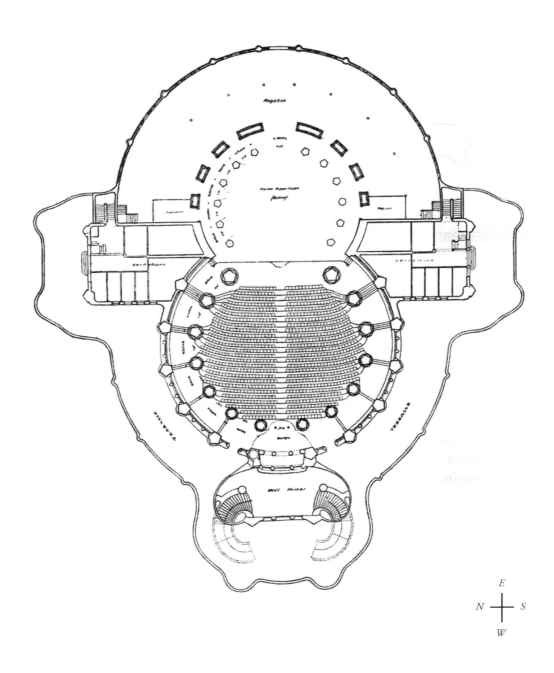

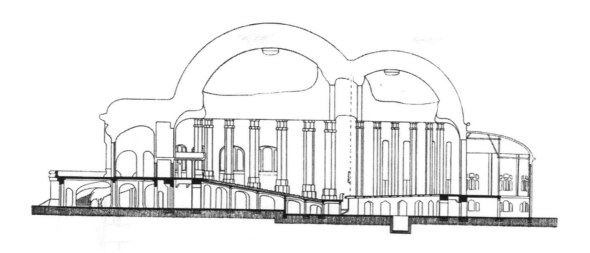

SLIDE 8: Here I've made a longitudinal section. You enter from the west through the anterooms. Here's the stage, and the main hall rising up from there, the rows of seats, the seven columns again, and here's the junction between the larger and the smaller cupolas, which was exceptionally challenging to construct. The storage rooms, the concrete foundation, the coat rooms. You enter here, and then here are the stairs; here's where you ascend and then the main doorway, through which you enter.

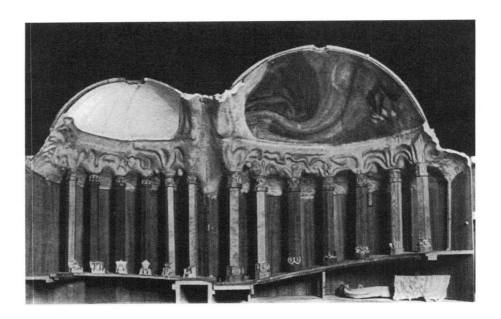

SLIDE 9: Here I have taken the liberty of showing you a longitudinal section of my original model. I originally modeled the whole building in 1913.[16] You see here first of all the great hall with its seven columns, the anterooms, here just barely indicated the inside of the larger cupola, which has been painted. Here under the smaller cupola you see all the capitals—in a moment I'll show them to you individually—and here above them the motifs of the architrave; here the motifs of the bases, each of which always proceeds from the other. There's only one axis of symmetry, the central axis of the building. There are no repetitions other than these symmetries of left and right.

---

16. For an overview of the many preparatory stages leading up to the construction of the first Goetheanum, see CW 284; *Rosicrucianism Renewed: The Unity of Art, Science, and Religion: The Theosophical Congress of Whitsun 1907* (Great Barrington, MA: SteinerBooks, 2007).

SLIDE 10: The west portal again, the main door above the terrace, with two side wings, which are necessary because the larger cupola weighs upon them.

SLIDE 11: Here is one of the wings. In the background you see the house of Dr. Grosheintz, a building made entirely of concrete with approximately fifteen rooms. It is a family residence, and I wanted to experiment with creating a residence starting from concrete as a building material, and then immersing myself in the qualities of this particular material. It was built near the Goetheanum for the person who donated the land to us.

You see here how I sought to metamorphose the motif [of the Goetheanum]. Everything about this building emerges like one leaf from another in a plant: it's the activity of metamorphosis in an artistic sense.

SLIDE 12:   Here is the northern wing.

SLIDE 13: And here you see the south wing head-on, from the south. You see here how the motif that's above the west entrance reappears in a completely different form. The outer form is completely different, but the underlying idea is the same. It's just like the plant, in which we might say that the colored blossom leaf is ideally the same as the lowest, green foliage leaf, even though it appears completely differently within the external metamorphosis of forms.

By entering empathetically, finding one's way into the metamorphosis—understanding it affectively rather than in abstract, intellectual terms—by giving oneself over to that, it's possible to intuit the organic design of the building. That's not something to be explained; rather, everything should present itself immediately in the act of viewing. When the building is finished, those who are well acquainted with the anthroposophical worldview, with the anthroposophical way of feeling, won't experience the building as in any way symbolic. Rather, they'll experience it as something that flows directly from the whole feeling I just described. Of course some people will say that it needs to flow from "the universally human," but this idea of something universally human—that's just a nebulous construct, a complete fantasy. The human is always concrete. Of course if you know nothing about Christianity, you can't understand the *Sistine Madonna*.[17] Anyone who lacked a real Christian sensibility would never understand *The Last Supper* in Santa Maria della Grazie in Milan.[18] Of course it's entirely the case that we can find our way into a given phenomenon via language. But apart from this, there's nothing symbolic anywhere in the building: all the forms differ from each other metamorphically.

---

17. Raphael's great masterpiece of 1512, which currently hangs in the *Gemäldegalerie* in Dresden.
18. Leonardo da Vinci's famous mural of 1495-1498.

Slide 14:   The corner of the south wing.

SLIDE 15: North wing of the west portal [viewed from the west].

SLIDE 16:   Here you have the south wing again, viewed from the southeast. Here above you see a substantially modified, metamorphosed variation of the motif that's also over the west entrance. All of these motifs are in various stages of metamorphosis, so that the design of the entire building has been executed organically. Likewise you would find, if you were to study the columns, that there's a single basic form which has been constantly metamorphosed. The building is like the human constitution, in which the cranial bones are metamorphoses of the vertebrae—indeed everything in the human organism is a series of metamorphic transformations, right down into the smallest details.

SLIDE 17:   The upper part of the south wing, seen from the terrace itself.

SLIDE 18:   Close-up of the lower door of the east entrance, at an earlier stage of construction.

SLIDE 19:   Here you see the east entrance, which leads to the storage rooms of the stage area. Because of the height of the flats, the door had to consist of two parts: the entry doors for daily use below, and a part that can be opened above, so that the tall flats can be carried in.

SLIDE 20: Here you see a bit of the stairs and part of the stairwell. Here is where you enter. You'd have come through the main entry downstairs in the concrete foundation and then climbed the stairs. Here you see the banister and here [on the right] there's a pillar. In this pillar you can see how I sought to give an organic form to a column that supports loads. You can see how I gave it the form that it needs to have vis-à-vis the exit across from it, because there's little weight to support along that axis; and on the other hand the form needs to show where it braces itself, where the whole weight of the staircase lies. Of course it's possible to form such a pillar geometrically. What I tried to do here, however, was to form everything as though it were ensouled, so that the building would appear *conscious* of its own loading and supporting. Every single curve, everything tailored precisely in an intuitive way to the place within the building in which it stands. Especially if you consider this motif here [on the left, at the base of the banister]: it's three interrelated semicircular canals. You can believe it or not, but it's true: if someone ascends the stairs here and then enters the main hall, then I think that they'll inevitably have a certain feeling. I said to myself: anyone going up there should have the sensation: inside there, my soul will be sheltered; there my soul will find the peace I need to take in the highest truths that human beings can strive to attain. So it was that the shaping of these three semicircular canals, situated perpendicular to each other in the three directions of spatial orientation, arose out of my own sensibility. If you ascend this staircase, then you can develop this feeling of *inner peace*. It's not an imitation—it really isn't that at all—but afterwards I remembered that the semicircular canals in the human ear also stand to each other in this same orientation. If they're damaged, then we fall into a faint: thus they're connected to the laws of balance. These forms didn't arise out of any kind of naturalistic desire to imitate; rather, they arose when I entered empathetically into the very forces that effect the orientations of the canals in the human ear.

SLIDE 21: Here you're entering from the west side, and you ascend the staircase. Here are the three semicircular canals, standing at right angles to one another. And here's that pillar again. So it is in life, of course—I've experienced it myself many times: if people in a particular city have seen an actor or an actress play a certain role, and then afterward someone else comes along who plays the part well, or better, or in a more interesting way than the first, then the performance that people already knew becomes the criterion for judging. If the newcomers did everything the same as in the earlier performance, then they were good; if they did it differently, then they were bad, no matter how good they actually were. And so people judge things such as this by comparing it with what they are accustomed to seeing. And when something like this has been put in place, they have no idea that it's standing where it is for a reason, supporting loads in ways that vary with its spatial relationships, or expressing such different qualities of supporting, and that all this has been drawn forth from the building as an organic whole. Some people found this pillar to be too thin, called it rachitic; others said that it resembled the foot of an elephant, but they didn't want to call it an "elephant's foot." And someone really made a fool of himself by drawing from the profundity of his artistic sensibility and then declaring it a "rachitic elephant's foot." That's what you get today if you delve down into elemental forces and create something new.

SLIDE 22: A radiator shield made of concrete.

SLIDE 23:   If you go up the stairs, you arrive here in this anteroom before entering the main hall. Now you begin to see the wooden building. This is the level of the concrete terrace, below it the concrete foundations. With this column you see how the capital with its curves conforms exactly to its surroundings—conforms not just in some merely schematic, spatial sense, but also dynamically. Movement towards the exit needs to express a different quality of supporting from what's expressed in the curves as we move toward the entrance, and yet again vis-à-vis the building itself, against which it needs to brace itself. Hence all of these wooden forms, capitals, architraves, and so forth had to be produced through many years of work by our friends in the Anthroposophical Society. All this is handwork, including for example the ceiling here, which also doesn't have a schematic form. Rather, all its surfaces have been shaped individually; they've been hollowed out differently depending upon the direction in which one moves away from the column. All of this has been shaped by the same law as that whereby for example the human ear is hollowed out differently in the front from the way it's hollowed out in the back, and so forth.

SLIDE 24:   Here you are in the main hall, looking up from the audience toward the columns. Here is the organ motif, here are the first two columns with their capitals. We'll come to the changed, metamorphosed capitals of the second, third, fourth column, and so forth; I'll show you that in detail right away. Always the architrave motifs above and the motifs of the bases below.

SLIDE 25: Here again, if you turn around within the main hall and look west, the organ motif above; the first and second columns with capitals left and right, the capitals and the architraves over them, with very simple forms. And now in the following slides I'll always show you a column and its successor, and then each column with its capital individually, so that you can see how each capital grows metamorphically out of its predecessor. And what I want to emphasize particularly in this way is also that the individual columns can't be judged in isolation. Rather, you always have to look to the entire sequence of columns in its evolving form.

SLIDE 26: This photo was taken during construction. The photos were taken at various times. We've been working on the building since 1913, when the foundation stone was laid, and the photos represent many different phases of construction.

Here I'm showing you the organ motif, the first two capitals, which are the simplest, with their architrave motifs above them. I'll show the following slides by first giving you an individual column, then the column together with its successor, and then the successor together with its successor, etc. Then you'll see how the life of these forms that feel themselves[19] unfolding evolves from one capital to the next and from one architrave motif to the next.

SLIDE 27: Here you see the first column by itself, the simplest motif imaginable. Inclining downward, rising, but conceived artistically at every point in a polyhedral-spherical form.

---

19. *das lebendige Sichfortfühlen*, a strong neologism in the German original, literally "the vital feeling-onward"

SLIDE 28:   Here you see the first motif: a capital with the architrave lying above it. Here's the second, emerging organically out of the first. The motif inclining downward from above is growing; in the process of growing it metamorphoses itself. Likewise the motif leading upward from below. You have to feel yourself merging as it were with forces that are active when one of the higher leaves of a plant, metamorphosed, emerges opposite the lower leaves. That's just how this initial, simple motif grows into one that's more complicated. The key is always to take in the whole sequence of motifs, because each always belongs together with the other. Indeed, all seven belong together; they constitute a whole.

SLIDE 29:   Here we see a close-up of the second column. Everywhere it's the same: the next motif proceeds metamorphically from the previous one.

SLIDE 30: The second and third columns. More complicated again, this third capital motif with the architrave motif above it. If you forgo trying to explain such forms symbolically, and stop coming at them with the intellect, and employ feeling instead, then you'll be able to see directly how one emerges from the other. Then this more complicated form actually yields itself up to your inner sensibility.

SLIDE 31: A close-up of the third column.

SLIDE 32:   The third and fourth columns—I mean their capitals with the architrave motif above them. Here you might be tempted to think that I sought to form a
kind of caduceus. But that's not what I tried to do. Rather I simply sought to
feel how these forms continue to grow after they meet, become more complicated, how they "become," and then the sensation of this caduceus-like
form arises all on its own. Likewise, if this [capital of the third column] grows
further—note how things simplify themselves from below upward and com-
plicate themselves from above downward—then this form arises [capital of the
fourth column], which I'll now show you by itself again.

SLIDE 33:   The fourth column.

SLIDE 34:   The fourth and fifth columns. What comes forth out of this form, if you conceive it as growing downward, is *this* form. It becomes simpler again. And what moves from below upward ramifies as it were into richer form towards the top. That's the remarkable thing: when thinking about evolution, people are led by a false belief, which has unfortunately become widespread, that things evolve from something simple to something more complicated and then to ever more complicated things until finally the most perfect thing is that which is most complicated. But if you enter into the evolutionary impulse in the right way, with an artistic sensibility, then you see that this isn't the case at all. Indeed, we have to proceed from the simple to the ever more complicated initially, but then we attain maximum complexity in the middle of the development. And when it proceeds from there on towards perfection, it becomes simpler again.

   This all came as a great surprise to me when I worked out the models for all these things. I had to transition from the simple to the more complex—as you see, here we've arrived at the fourth and fifth columns, so roughly in the middle of the seven columnar forms—and then I had to let the middle phase be the most complicated, and then transition to the simpler. And if I look back at the way in which nature herself creates, then I find this to be the case with the human eye as well. Although it's the most perfect organ, the eye isn't the most complicated. In the [anatomy of the] eyes of certain lower forms of animals we encounter the fan-like comb [of some birds] or the xiphoid process [of some fish].[20] The eyes of certain lower biological forms are in some regards more complicated than the more perfect human organ. And so it's also not the case in nature that evolution proceeds from the simple to the more complicated and then to the ever more complicated, but rather, if we pursue the matter further, we return to simpler forms again. The more perfect forms are simpler again. And so it is that in a creative process such as ours, the formal evolution we have just described emerges as an artistic necessity.

SLIDE 35:   The fifth column by itself.

---

20. This sentence seems to echo Otto Thilo's *Die Augen der Thiere* [*The Eyes of Animals*] (1899), where these unusual anatomical terms (*Fächer* and *Schwertfortsatz*) appear in close proximity. Steiner's point is that the human eye does not contain these more complicated inner structures. Thilo's anatomical drawings vividly confirm Steiner's contention.

SLIDE 36:   Now the fifth and sixth columns. You see that here [in the fifth] the capital is still relatively complicated; as it develops further, it becomes simpler again: so that this sixth capital, although it is more perfectly formed, nobler, is simpler again. Likewise the motif in the architrave.

SLIDE 37:   Close-up of the sixth column.

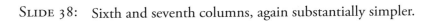

SLIDE 38:   Sixth and seventh columns, again substantially simpler.

SLIDE 39:   Close-up of the seventh column, again simplified.

SLIDE 40: This is the seventh column, the architrave motif, here's the break between the main hall and the stage. The curtain is in here. Then the first column under the small cupola, and here we enter into the space beneath the small cupola.

We've finished going over the sequence of columns in the main hall. Now I'll show you the sequence of the motifs on the bases, which have likewise grown out of each other metamorphically and organically.

SLIDE 41:   Now I will show you the base motifs in sequence. First base.

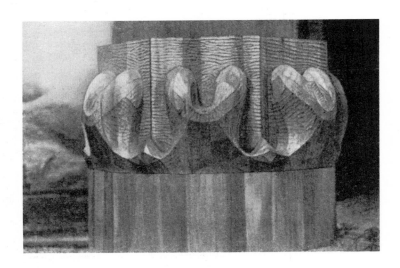

SLIDE 42:   Each proceeds metamorphically from the foregoing motif. Second base.

SLIDE 43:   The metamorphosis progresses. If you enter into them with your feeling, it's always the same: the metamorphosis inclines downward and new forms arise, then broaden out. Third base.

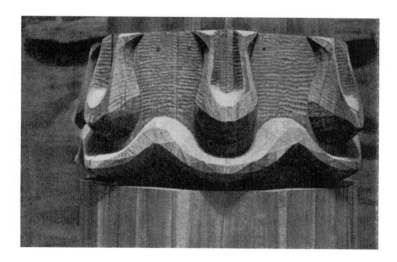

SLIDE 44:   More complicated again. And now we begin to see a simplification of the figures on the bases, as we move towards greater perfection. Fourth base.

SLIDE 45: Another base motif. You can't enter in here through intellectual speculation: you have to feel the necessity of the further development artistically. Fifth base.

SLIDE 46: If you conceive of the motif in a modified form, this is the result. Sixth base.

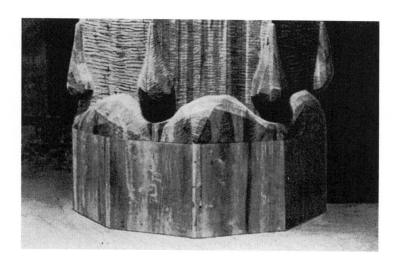

SLIDE 47: This seventh base figure is relatively simple again.

SLIDE 48:   Here you're looking into the stage from the audience. You can see the last columns of the main hall, then columns and architraves of the space under the small cupola. That's the conclusion of the main hall; here you have the middle of the space under the small cupola. Here a kind of architrave has been formed between the two center columns of the smaller space. This isn't any kind of symbolic figure. If you want to find a pentagram in it, well, you can find one in every flower with five petals. What we've done [in this figure] is synthesize all the lines and curves that are distributed among the individual columns. The ceiling of the smaller cupola has been covered with paintings. I'll say more about these paintings later in my lecture.

SLIDE 49: The first two columns and architraves under the smaller cupola. As you see, again we haven't just repeated the capitals of the main hall. Rather, they correspond to the architectural idea underlying the whole building. Since this space is smaller, each individual organ needs to be smaller within its organic context, and to have different forms. We've adhered to that principle in the shaping of this whole space as well.

SLIDE 50: Here you see again the view into the stage, the two last columns of the main hall; the same motif you've seen from other aspects—and here the stage under the smaller cupola. Of course the paintings aren't really visible here, but at least you can see how they're situated relative to the other elements.

SLIDE 51:   Individual columns of the stage beneath the smaller cupola. Here's the break. If you cross from west to east, this is what you see on your left. Here's the architrave of the stage beneath the smaller cupola. The bases of the columns have been transformed into seats.

The Architectural Idea of the First Goetheanum   73

52

53

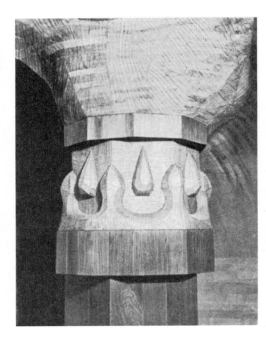

54

55

56

57

SLIDE 52:   The first column on the stage.

SLIDE 53:   In accordance with the principle of growth, the next one exhibits a more complicated form.

SLIDE 54:   And the next one is more complicated again.

SLIDE 55:   Now the tendency is towards simplification, but the simplification is only apparent: what we're really seeing is an outgrowth.

SLIDE 56:   The columns grow forth out of each other metamorphically.

SLIDE 57:   The next and last column.

SLIDE 58:   And now we come already to the two columns that bound the east end. Here we have the carving of the east end. Let me say that here the forms can be felt more easily than they can be seen.[21] If you look carefully, you'll find that in the carving here at the eastern end, everything that was contained in the other forms of the columns and architraves is synthesized, of course in a way that's been metamorphosed to fit the vaulting of this space. Above it is a cinquefoil. Anyone who wishes can project a pentagram onto this shape, of course, just as someone can imagine it as a natural plant with five blossoms or leaves. A symbolist[22] would have placed some kind of pentagram there. Only by suffusing forms completely with spirit can we attain what we're striving to achieve here: not blatant symbols, but rather a creative shaping within the forms. But it has to be a shaping of the forms such that they're animated by the same spirit that also lives within the ideas of our worldview. Here the spirit isn't expressed by this or that symbolic form; rather, these forms have within them real, inner forces of growth.

---

21. This anticipates the artist Joseph Beuys' saying: "one hears a sculpture before one sees it."
22. *ein Symboliker*. Steiner is thinking of the older Theosophists with whom he had worked for many years, and certainly not of avant-garde groups such as the Russian Symbolists, some of whom (notably Bely and Woloschin) were members of his circle who helped to build the first Goetheanum. "Allegory" might have been a more appropriate term for the kind of art Steiner is decrying here.

58

59

SLIDE 59: Here you see the individual forms of the [northern part of the] architrave somewhat more clearly.

SLIDE 60: A detail from the opposite side of the stage, under the smaller cupola; hence they're mirror images of the forms we just saw.

SLIDE 61: Here the orders of the columns would continue on the right and on the left. Here we're in the middle of the east end right beneath the smaller cupola, right where all the lines, all the curves are brought together in the most various forms; all the lines and curves elsewhere in the building are synthesized here. This is a kind of architrave, intermediate architrave; underneath it will stand the Group, about which I'll say more, a wooden sculpture nine-and-a-half meters tall, the middle figure of which depicts a kind of Representative of Humanity. Above it the space defined by the smaller cupola.

60

61

SLIDE 62:   The massive speaker's rostrum, carved out of wood.[23]

23. This is the rostrum that stands in the second Goetheanum, a reproduction carved by Oswald Dubach after the original burned together with the first Goetheanum.

SLIDE 63 (*page 83*):

And now we come to the painting of the ceiling of the smaller cupola.[24] At present I can show you only the painting of one part of the ceilings, that of the smaller cupola in particular, because the painting of the larger cupola hasn't been fully accomplished yet. But here on the ceiling of the smaller cupola we've been successful to some degree in our experiment, which was to realize what one of the characters in my Mystery Dramas said about the new painting[25]: that form should be the work of color.[26] That is to say, we really should try to rise up to an experience of the world of color as such.

If we survey the world of color, we find that it's actually a totality of sorts, a world unto itself. And if we enter empathetically, in an entirely living way, into the realm of color, then we might say that red and blue and yellow converse with each other.[27] Something becomes totally alive within the realm of color and we come to know a world of color that's a being in itself.[28] Then all drawing ceases; then one experiences drawing as something that is ultimately

---

24. See the early color photos of the cupola paintings in Appendix 2.

25. "The new painting" is clearly a reference to the experiments of groups such as The Blue Rider in Munich, who were deeply influenced by Steiner's teachings. See e.g. the now-classic study by Sixten Ringbom, *Sounding Cosmos: A Study in the Spiritualism of Kandinsky and the Genesis of Abstract Painting*, Acta academiae Aboensis, ser. A, v. 38, No. 2 (Abo Akademi, 1970), and also his articles "Kandinsky und das Okkulte" [Kandinsky and the Occult] and "Die Steiner-Annotationen Kandinskys" [Kandinsky's Marginalia in Publications by Steiner] in Armin Zweite, ed., *Kandinsky und München: Begegnungen und Waldlungen 1896-1914* (München: Prestel-Verlag, 1982), pp. 85-105. The hero of Steiner's four Mystery Dramas, performed in Munich from 1910-1913, is a painter named Johannes Thomasius. His monologue at the beginning of Scene Three of the second drama, *The Soul's Probation*, is an eloquent evocation of the spirit that animated the "new painting" in Munich right before the war.

26. *daß die Form der Farbe Werk sein soll.* These words are spoken by Strader as he marvels at Johannes Thomasius' painted portrait of Capesius in Scene Eight of Steiner's first Mystery Drama, *The Portal of Initiation*. It is a riddle and a challenge to the skeptical scientist how the artist's use of color can capture spiritual realities. Strader's long, anguished response to Thomasius' portrait is a perfect little inverse manifesto on the new painting, worthy of Kandinsky, and worth quoting at length:

> My friend's soul power shines
> out of these eyes, though they are merely painted.
> The scholar's thoughtfulness
> lives on this brow;
> the innate warmness of his words
> streams from each color tone
> with which your brush
> has solved this riddle.
> O all these colors, – they are only surface,
> and yet they're not.
> It is as if they're only visible
> to make themselves invisible to me.
> These forms,
> emerging as the colors' interplay,
> speak of the spirit's weaving.
> Indeed they speak of much
> which they themselves are not.*

*Rudolf Steiner, *Four Mystery Dramas* (Great Barrington, MA: SteinerBooks, 2014), p. 130.

a lie. For, what is the line of the horizon, actually? If I draw it with a pencil, then I'm actually setting down something false. Below is the green surface of the sea; above is the blue surface of the vault of the heavens. Wherever I lay down color, form—the line—emerges as the boundary of the color.[29]

And so it really is possible to draw forth out of color itself everything that we want to bring to the wall figuratively in the form of painting.[30] Don't be deceived by the presence of figures, indeed of figures from the history of culture. For me, the most important thing in the painting of this smaller cupola was not to paint this or that motif on the wall, but rather to show for example that here there's an orange patch in various shades of orange. And then out of those nuanced colors arose the figure of the child. And here the most important

---

27. Cf. van Gogh's letter to his brother Theo of October 28, 1885, in which he praises the art of Jules Dupré "for what enormous diversity of mood he expressed in symphonies of color. Now a marine, with the most delicate blue-greens and broken blue and all kinds of pearly tones, then again an autumn landscape, with the foliage from deep wine-red to vivid green, from bright orange to dark havana, with other colors again in the sky, in grays, lilacs, blues, whites, forming a further contrast with the yellow leaves. Then again a sunset in black, in violet, in fiery red. Then again more fantastic, like the corner of a garden by him that I saw and have never forgotten; black in the shadow, white in the sun, bright green, a fiery red, and then again a dark blue, a bituminous greenish brown and a light brownish yellow. Truly colors that can have quite a lot to say to one another."

28. *wesenhaft*. This predicate adjective might be translated as "substantial" or "substantive," but it is clear from Steiner's many other writings on the arts that he means this term in the strongest possible sense: colors are spiritual realities, the deeds of higher beings. Cf. Goethe's famous assertion in the "Preface" of his *Theory of Color* that colors are "the deeds and sufferings of light" (Johann Wolfgang von Goethe, *Scientific Studies*, vol. 12 of the Suhrkamp Edition [in English], ed. and trans. Douglas Miller [New York: Suhrkamp Publishers, 1988], p. 158).

29. Cf. Wassily Kandinsky, *Concerning the Spiritual in Art* (New York: Dover, 1977), p. 29: "Form, in the narrow sense, is nothing but the separating line between surfaces of color. That is its outer meaning. But it also has an inner meaning, of varying intensity, and, properly speaking, *form is the outward expression of this inner meaning.*"

30. *wesenhaft als Malerei*; cf. the sentence in the following paragraph that places *das Wesenhafte and die Gestalt* ("the figure") in apposition, and also Steiner's use of the same term in the previous sentence, which together imply a profound aesthetics of painting: the motifs, the formal "figures" of the painting are part of a continuum of spiritual activity that has its origins in the deeds of higher beings. See Kandinsky's essay "On the Question of Form" [*Über die Formfrage*], published originally as part of *The Blue Rider Almanac*. Kandinsky's term for this inner life of colors is their "sound" [*Klang*]:

> Form is always temporal, i.e. relative, because it is only the medium that is necessary today, within which today's revelation makes itself known, resounds [*klingt*]. Hence the *Klang* is the soul of form, which can come alive only through the *Klang* and exerts its effects from the inside outward. *Form is the outer expression of the inner content.**

* Wassily Kandinsky and Franz Marc, *The Blaue Reiter Almanac* (New York: Viking, 1974), p. 149; translation modified slightly by F.A.

63

thing was that blue was set down next to it: the result was the figure that you
are about to see. Everywhere the figures, the beings that you see, have been
drawn forth entirely from the color. So here you have a flying child in shades
of orange. Here's where the larger and smaller cupolas are joined, and so this is
the first thing you see upon the ceiling of the smaller cupola. But in looking at
these motifs it's best for you to feel them. It's best if you say to yourself: actually I can't see anything here; I have to see it chromatically. For truly everything
here was conceived and felt and painted directly out of color.

SLIDE 64: Here you see the only word in the entire building. Otherwise you won't see any inscriptions; everything has been shaped artistically, in terms of forms. But here you find the word "I" [*Ich*]. Out of the color blue has emerged a kind of a Faust figure, which is to say, a man of the sixteenth century.[31] Here the whole problem of knowledge as it confronts modern humanity has been given a form that arises directly out of a feeling for color. When this problem of knowledge is depicted visually in the usual way today, the result is a feeling that's merely abstract. If we confront in the right way everything that modern science has yielded in the form of natural laws, then they penetrate right into our souls. But this can't happen so long as we contemplate things only as bookish theorizers. Faustian striving, complete immersion in the mysteries of the universe, is what we need in order to be fully human, in order to become conscious of our human dignity. In Faust we have such a striving individuality, an archetype of the human striving to know, an archetype that really does strive forth in the person of Faust out of the mysterious, mystical blue, that strives for the fully conscious "I," the "I" that calls itself forth in the word—indeed, ancient languages include the "I" within the word.[32] Looking to the era of Faust we're justified in allowing a single word to arise, even though there's otherwise not a single word, inscription—there's nothing of that sort anywhere in the building; everything has been expressed in artistic forms. If we really immerse ourselves in the mysteries of the universe, then two images place themselves next to the human being striving for knowledge: the child, which is to say birth, and the other end of life, death.

---

31. Steiner's main engagements with Goethe's *Faust* are collected in three volumes of his Collected Works, all from SteinerBooks: CW 272, *Anthroposophy in the Light of Goethe's Faust* (2015); CW 273, *Goethe's Faust in the Light of Anthroposophy* (2016); and CW 22, *Goethe's Spirituality as Revealed in Goethe's* Faust *and* The Fairy Tale of the Green Snake and the Beautiful Lily (forthcoming).

32. As in, for example, the Latin paradigm verb *amo*, "I love," which is first person in the absence of a pronoun.

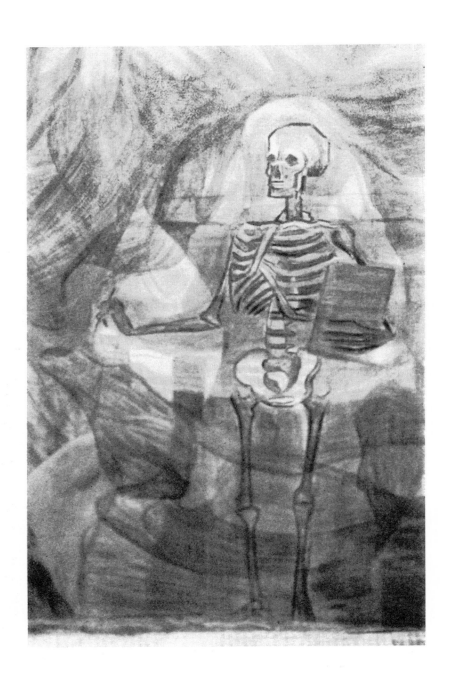

SLIDE 65 & 66:

The figure of Faust whom you just saw is above this figure of Death [Slide 65, opposite], and just next to this flying child [above]. [Death] in brownish-black, Faust in blue, the child in various hues of orange-yellow.

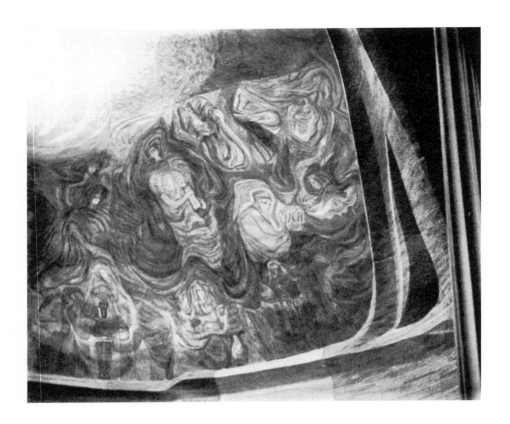

SLIDE 67: Here you see juxtaposed: the skeleton below, Faust, this child that you've seen in detail, above a kind of inspirer, an angelic figure, which I'll show you by itself later. Here other figures join the group. What arose out of the colored surfaces that I wanted to bring to this place was, as I said before, the need to depict here the striving of humanity over the last few centuries. Here we see the striving within Greek culture. You'll see this in detail later in the lecture.

Slide 68: The genius in blue, above the figure of Faust, as though inspiring the figure of Faust from above.

SLIDE 69: A kind of Athena figure, called forth out of a brownish-orange with light
yellow. This is the means whereby Greek culture gained a living relationship
to knowledge, and a living relationship to the entire world. This figure here is
inspired by a kind of Apollo figure [Slide 70], just as Faust was previously inspired by his angel. This Athena figure transports us back to Ancient Greece.[33]

33. Steiner saw earlier human cultures as having been inspired directly by the spiritual world. For a
concise and elegant treatment of this idea that pervades all of Steiner's work, see CW 15: *The Spiritual Guidance of the Individual and Humanity* (Hudson, New York: Anthroposophic Press, 1991),
and also the early chapters of Owen Barfield's magisterial study *Saving the Appearances: A Study in
Idolatry* (London: Faber, 1957; rpt. Wesleyan University Press).

SLIDE 70:   Apollo the Inspirer. Here I paid special attention to this bright yellow; I sought to create this Apollo figure right out of the color itself. This bright yellow—I tried to give it a certain radiant quality in the technique I employed.

SLIDE 71:   Here you see two beings who inspire the Egyptian initiate as he seeks to know and sense the world. It's been done in somewhat darker colors: I would call this hue brownish-reddish. The Egyptian initiate beneath them was done in the same hues.

SLIDE 72: The Egyptian initiate, hence the counterpart within those very ancient times to what Faust represents for us today in his striving for knowledge.

SLIDE 73:   Here you see two figures to whom anthroposophy must always give specific names, because they constantly recur. Please don't associate this with any kind of nebulous mysticism; it really is just a matter of needing a terminology. Just as one speaks of the north and south poles of a magnet and so forth, I speak of the Luciferic and the Ahrimanic.[34] If we attempt to form a picture of human nature as a whole, we find that it simply isn't possible, no matter what human faculties we might bring to bear. We simply cannot build up a comprehensive picture out of our own individuality alone. We have a larger polarity within us. On the one hand, we have within us something that continually tempts us to strive in the direction of enthusiastic, false mysticism and false theory; we have within us something that's always striving to rise up over our own heads into unreal, groundless, nebulous realms. This is what I call the Luciferic. And then on the other hand there's everything that makes us philistines, that predisposes us toward the Spirit of Gravity[35]: the Ahrimanic, which is depicted here together with its shadow. The Luciferic has been worked up out of yellowish-red, the Ahrimanic out of yellowish-brown. It's the dualistic aspect of human nature. This polarity expresses itself physically and physiologically as well: Ahriman is the aspect of human nature that causes us to age, and makes us sclerotic, calcified, ossified; the Luciferic is the aspect that expresses itself in everything associated with fever, pleurisy—everything that makes us develop in the direction of excessive warmth. Human nature always represents an equilibrium between these two. Until we see it as a balance between these two forces, between the Luciferic and the Ahrimanic, we haven't begun to comprehend human nature.

---

34. Rudolf Steiner spoke often about the dual nature of evil, ascribing its source to suprasensible beings he calls Lucifer and Ahriman. For an excellent discussion of Steiner's ideas as applied to Goethe's *Faust*, see Alan P. Cottrell, *Goethe's View of Evil and the Search for a New Image of Man in our Time* (Edinburgh: Floris, 1982). Mephistopheles in Goethe's *Faust* exhibits traits of both beings by turns, and Steiner was critical of Goethe for having conflated them. Lucifer and Ahriman also appear as characters in Steiner's own expressionist Mystery Dramas (1910-1913): see CW 14, Rudolf Steiner, *Four Mystery Dramas*, (Great Barrington, MA: SteinerBooks, 2014). Lucifer might be termed the "red devil," who tempts humans to sin on the side of *superbia*: pride, anger, egotism, erotic passions, etc. "Ahriman" is a traditional name for a black demon, beginning with the Zoroastrian figure Angra Mainyu, opponent of the Sun God Ahura Mazda. Ahriman's temptations are those of *acedia*: laziness, greed, and denial of the Spirit generally. Steiner argues that the assaults of these beings are providential: only by overcoming their resistance and holding them in proper balance can humanity become inwardly strong enough to develop genuine freedom, knowledge, and love.

35. *der Geist der Schwere*. Steiner has borrowed this epithet from Nietzsche, who bestowed it upon the opponent of his hero, Zarathustra.

Above all, however, I have confronted the Germanic-Central European culture, which traces its roots back to Ancient Persia, with an awareness of this duality. Hence also the Central European thinker, who has the child here—we shall look more closely at this thinker. He's inspired by the duality of the Luciferic-Ahrimanic; his destiny as a thinker is that, in a way that is inwardly tragic, he has to come to terms with this philosophical destiny.

This kind of dualism was expressed again in the smaller figure that's centaur-like. I painted it during the War, and, well, one does just have one's own private thoughts. I see the unfortunate web of Woodrow Wilson's Fourteen Points as having been spun out of an abstract metamorphosis of just this dualism.

Here in Switzerland I've spoken over and over about the destructiveness of these Fourteen Points for the world.[36] Hence I indulged in the private pleasure of immortalizing Mr. and Mrs. Wilson in these figures. But let's not dwell on it; it's something of little significance really.

---

36. Wilson's program promoted nationalism at a time when Steiner was calling for a truly international economy and a cosmopolitan cultural life that transcended political boundaries. On Steiner's social theories, see e.g. CW 24, *The Renewal of the Social Organism*, (Spring Valley, NY: Anthroposophic Press, 1985) generally, and specifically the articles "The International Economy and the Threefold Social Order" (pp. 15-23) and "International Aspects of the Threefold Social Order" (pp. 58-65).

SLIDE 74 (*page 98*):

Here you see a detail of the figure of Ahriman and the shadow above it. In psychic terms, this figure represents everything that drives us as human beings to become materialistic, philistine, and pedantic. It represents how we would be if—in exaggerated terms now—we had only intellect and no heart, if all of our inner faculties were directed by the intellect. And if we were so unfortunate as to lose balance within our outer bodies, then the appearance of those outer bodies would actually be determined by the state of our souls; it would be the direct expression of our inner life. Everyone whose feeling was materialistic, whose sensations were materialistic and pedantic, anyone who was almost entirely consumed by intellectuality would look this way externally. Such people are naturally protected against such a thing happening because their bodies don't always follow their souls, but this is how their souls look if one looks at them, if one senses them in a corporeal way.

SLIDE 75 (*page 99*):

The Luciferic figure, worked up out of yellow hues, from yellow into brightness. This is what forms inside us if we become imbalanced on the side of enthusiasm, on the side of theosophy, if we want to grow beyond our own heads. You can see this formation among members of the anthroposophical movement as well, people whose astral head has grown half a meter taller than their physical head so that they can look down on everyone else. This is the other extreme, the other pole within human nature.

SLIDE 76: Here below is a figure who represents a sort of Germanic initiate, the German thinker in his tragedy, which is that a duality has an especially strong effect on him: the Luciferic and the Ahrimanic; and then, as a complement to that [tragedy], the naiveté of the child. This is the image that presented itself to my sensibility as an artist. The initiate was worked up out of brown-yellow, the child was kept bright yellow.

SLIDE 77:   Here is a detail from the same image, magnified somewhat.

SLIDE 78: Here we're closer to the center of the cupola. Here's where this man would stand with the child, and more toward the middle are these two figures, which are one, however. What's meant here is not the current Russian culture—or unculture we should rather say, which is so destructive of both humanity and nature. I mean the germ of the future that dwells within Russian culture. At present it's merely overshadowed by something imported from the West—something that must disappear from the earth as soon as possible lest it drag all of Europe into the abyss. But at the foundation of Russian folk culture lies something that surely will come in the future. All that is meant to be expressed by this figure, which has only its double [*Doppelgänger*] next to it. What lives within Russian culture always has a kind of a double alongside it. Every Russian drags his shadow around with him. Whenever we see a Russian, we actually see two beings: the Russian who dreams, who is actually flying a yard above the ground, and then in addition the shadow. Many possibilities for the future are latent here.[37] Hence this characteristic angelic figure, which is painted out of the color blue, out of the most various nuances of blue. Above is a kind of a centaur, a kind of a flying centaur.

---

37. See also Steiner's comments on Russian culture as depicted here in his lecture of December 30, 1921: "Towards the middle of the east end, we have this double figure. This figure represents what will someday grow out of the chaotic elements of Russian culture. In Russian souls we have as it were the preparation for the future state of the human soul, even if they must work their way through a wide array of chaotic conditions meanwhile. There human nature is still such that basically each person carries around a second person within, and this is something that reveals itself to the clairvoyant eye. Every Russian actually carries around his own shadow inside him. The result is a kind of dull inner presentiment that feels like inspiration, a situation we have tried to depict in this constellation of the blue figure here, and on the other side in the orange angelic figure and in the centaur-like figure above it. We tried to capture the relationship that the Russian's foreshadowing of the future state of the human soul currently has to nature and the world." This heretofore untranslated lecture has been included in GA 288, forthcoming from SteinerBooks.

SLIDE 79:   Here in this image, everything remains indefinite, even the star-like motif above this Russian, who bears the double within.

SLIDE 80:   At this point we've passed the midline. This is the same centaur figure—looking to the east, it's on the left—as the earlier one, which was to the right of the midline. This angelic figure is symmetrical to the one you just saw. But this figure has been worked up out of yellow-orange. Beneath it would be the Russian figure with the double, but symmetrical to the one that was just shown.

SLIDE 81:

Now we're standing in the middle of the stage, beneath the smaller cupola. Again the Russian motif on the other side. Here next to it you see the Ahriman figure lying in a cave; here above, the Representative of Humanity. You can think of him as Christ. Out of my inner vision, I formed him very much as a Christ figure. Flashes of lightning go out from his right hand, and they coil around Ahriman like snakes. The raised arm and hand moves toward Lucifer, who has been painted in reddish-yellow hues.

SLIDE 82:

Here you see the Lucifer figure somewhat more clearly—the Christ figure would be below it, reaching upward with his arm. Here's the countenance, worked up out of reddish-yellow hues. So the Luciferic influence is that within us which strives to expand beyond our heads, the forces of enthusiasm. It's a power that alienates us from our true humanity, making us otherworldly and ungrounded.

SLIDE 83:

Ahriman in his cave. His head is entwined by the snaking bolts of lightning that emanate from the hand of Christ, who is standing above. Here the wing, the brown-yellow patch, is shading over more into brown, and in places shading into blue-black as one moves downward.

Slide 84: The painted head of Christ between Ahriman and Lucifer—between the images that I just showed. You see that I've tried to depict Christ without a beard: it's only since the end of the fifth and sixth centuries that images of Christ have a beard. Of course nobody needs to believe me, but this is the image of Christ that revealed itself to me clairvoyantly, and so He must be depicted without a beard. And so above, on the ceiling of the cupola, Christ has been painted between Ahriman and Lucifer, and later (it's a long way from being finished) the wooden statue of The Group will stand. It's nine-and-a-half meters tall. In the middle will stand the Representative of Humanity, Christ, with His right arm extending downward, and His left arm reaching upward—standing in such a way that this pose seems to represent incarnated Love itself, having interposed itself between Lucifer and Ahriman. Christ shows no aggression toward either of them. Christ stands there like Love that has become embodied within itself. Lucifer doesn't fall because Christ causes him to fall, but rather because he cannot bear the proximity of Christ, the proximity of the Being who is Love incarnate.

Slide 85:   [Note by Marie Steiner: The wooden sculpture of The Group as it now stands inside the second Goetheanum. The work was almost done, but not completely finished when Rudolf Steiner laid down his chisel. It has been left in the state it had attained when he last put his hand to it.]

86

Toward a New Theory of Architecture

87

88

89

SLIDES 86-89:   These images show the Representative of Humanity, who stands in the middle of the wooden grouping. But I want to state expressly, nowhere is it going to say: "That's the Christ." Rather, that realization will be left entirely to your feelings. You'll need to feel it in the forms, in the work of art itself. Except for the single word "I" that I mentioned previously, there's no inscription anywhere in the whole building.

SLIDE 90: This is taken from the left side of the wooden statue (although what you're seeing here is actually the plastiline model). Here's Lucifer striving upward, and above him is a being of the rocks. This being forms himself gradually out of the rock; he is, as it were, the rock that has been metamorphosed into an organ. And then here's Lucifer; here's where Christ would stand; here's the other Lucifer, and that is a rock-being of sorts. I was so bold as to make it quite asymmetrical (asymmetries play a role with such beings in any case), because of the way in which the group was composed. I didn't proceed by taking figures and then putting them together to compose a whole—no, first I conceived the whole, and only then did I draw the particulars out of that whole. And so it was that a face at the top left needs to display a symmetry that's different from the symmetry at the top right. It was a risky thing to work with such asymmetries, but I hope that you'll find it to have been justified artistically when you eventually see and can feel it within the larger context of the architectural theory of the building as a whole.

SLIDE 91: From a somewhat different aspect: the being just discussed, and beneath it the Luciferic being, the head of this Luciferic being from the wooden sculpture of The Group.

SLIDE 92: Here we see the model of the head of Ahriman. This is the original model in wax that I created in 1915. What I tried to do here was to imagine how the human head would look if the only forces at work within it were the forces of aging, the sclerotic, calcifying forces. Or, in psychological terms, if only those forces were present that make us into philistines, pedants, materialists—the forces that make us want to intellectualize everything. If humans had no hearts within their souls, but only intellect, then this is the physiognomy that they would present. We can't come to know human nature if we describe it in the way that conventional anatomy and physiology do. Then we arrive only at a one-sided knowledge of human nature. We have to rise up to an artistic comprehension of the human form: only then do we begin to learn what works and lives within human nature; only then do we begin to comprehend the forces that are really at work within us. We'll never understand human nature if we go about it academically, reducing it to anatomy and physiology. We have to rise up to the level of art. And the heart of such artistic cognition is to recognize the truth expressed by Goethe when he says: "As soon as nature has begun to unveil her open secret to us, we begin to feel an irresistible longing for her most worthy interpreter, the arts."[38]

It's not just the abstract word, not just the abstract idea and the abstract concept that reveal something of the real forces of nature, of that which is contained within the mysteries of nature; these are revealed by the image as well. We have to rise up to the level of art: otherwise we can't come to know nature.

Our building has every right to call itself "Goetheanum" because such a Goethean attempt to understand nature strives to attain knowledge of the entire cosmos in that way as well. Goethe says: Art is a special way of uncovering the mysteries of nature, which never could have been revealed without art.[39]

That's my original model of Ahriman-Mephistopheles. Mephistopheles is only a later metamorphosis of Ahriman, who signifies what I just described physiologically, psychically, and spiritually. This model was the prototype for all Ahriman figures. I formed it originally in 1915 with my wooden model of The Group in mind.

---

38. *Maxims and Reflections*, #720
39. A paraphrase of *Maxims and Reflections*, #719: "Beauty is a manifestation of secret natural laws, which would have remained hidden from us forever had they not appeared as art."

SLIDE 93: The figure of Ahriman, carved from wood, from the lower portion of the wooden sculpture of The Group.

SLIDE 94: Detail from the plastiline model, middle portion. Head of Ahriman.

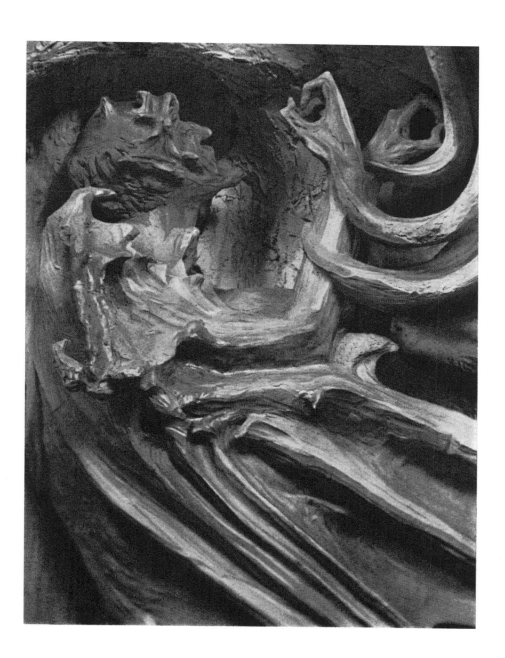

SLIDE 95: The figure of Lucifer above, standing, here the chest, wing-like. You really need to enter empathetically into the whole life of nature in order to sculpt something like this figure of Lucifer. Here you can't symbolize, or allegorize, or ponder, or cast what you have thought out into earlier forms. Rather, you really need to enter deeply into the ways in which nature creates; you really need to get to know the nature of the human larynx, the human ribcage, the lung, the organ of hearing, and then the stunted tools for flying that humans have in both shoulder blades. All of that needs to be synthesized, because we humans would look completely different if we weren't formed with an intellect, if the heart were to hypertrophy and overgrow everything else. Then the heart, the organs of hearing, wing-like organs, would all be one and the same. Anyone who grants validity not just to naturalism, but also to the ideal and spiritual sides of all beings, will begin to see how art such as this also reveals the mysteries of the world and of existence too in a Goethean sense.

At the top you see the hands of this asymmetrical rock-being.

SLIDE 96: Here you see a building that stands in the vicinity of the Goetheanum. We had to erect this building originally so that we'd have a place to carry out a kind of glass etching. Glass windows have been set into the wooden outer walls of the main hall [of the Goetheanum] between each pair of columns. These windows haven't been conceived in the mode of traditional stained glass. Rather, they're the product of a new artistic technique that I'd like to call *glass etching*. Glass panes of a uniform color are etched out using an electric drill with a diamond bit, so that the artist works here in the same way as an engraver etches a plate, except that the format is much larger. So the artist is scratching the motif out of the monotone glass, working it in such a way that light shines through the motif. That's how we obtained these glass windows, which have various colors, so that there's a harmonious effect. When you enter the building, you come first to one glass color, then to another, in a sequence of specific color harmonies. These glass windows had to be cut here on site, and this building was raised for that purpose. Right down to the doorway and the steps leading up to it, every detail has been formed individually. We didn't even use commercial locks of the conventional kind: instead, we devised a special kind of lock just for this building. That's what I mean when I say it's been formed individually right down into the smallest detail.

SLIDE 97: The doorway to the house just shown; beneath it the stairs made of concrete.

SLIDE 98:

And now let's look again at the Heating Plant; I already told you how it came to be. Here we're looking at it more or less straight on. Lots of people are very annoyed at it. We've tried to create a form using concrete, which is a very difficult material. Perhaps this is something we'll be able to perfect over time. What such people don't stop to consider is what would be standing here otherwise: a red brick chimney! Now tell me that would actually be more beautiful!

SLIDE 99 (*page 134*): Here you see one of these glass windows [photographed in the atelier while being etched]. This one has been executed in green. The motifs here have been drawn forth from green panes that are entirely the same color. The result of the engraving is a kind of a musical score, if you will. It becomes a work of art only when it's in place and the sun is shining through it. So the artist doesn't complete the work of art, but rather only a musical score: when the sun shines through, then the result of this etching is that, together with the sunbeams shining through, the actual work of art is completed. This process underscores a principle that arises out of the architectural theory underlying the whole complex in Dornach. Here it's been given physical expression.

Right down to its foundations, the building in Dornach has been constructed according to an architectural theory very different from that underlying other buildings. The walls of previous buildings have all been walls that enclose, and that's how they've been conceived artistically. But none of the walls in Dornach were conceived that way: all the walls here are meant to be aesthetically transparent rather than opaque, so that when you're inside, you don't feel cut off. The artistic motifs open up all the walls, as it were, to the whole, wide cosmos, and you enter this building with the consciousness that you are not inside a building, but rather within the cosmos itself. The walls are transparent. And in the glass windows this principle has been carried right down into the physical material: they become works of art only when the sun shines through them. Only when it meets the ray of sunlight does the product of the artist's hand become something artistic.

SLIDE 100 (*page 135*): Here's another example of our windows, which have been called forth out of monotone panes of glass. Because of these windows, the space is illumined with rays of light swimming into each other. And especially if you enter the room during the morning hours, in full sunlight, the effect of the glass windows is a strong feeling of *inwardness*—not in any nebulous way, but in the best sense of the word. You receive an impression, a representation of the inwardness of human and cosmic existence. Inside the Greek temple stood a house,[40] but not a house of the kind that any human being would ever enter! The pronaos perhaps, to leave an offering, but never the cella! The cella was the house of the god. And buildings in the Gothic style—not just churches, but secular buildings as well—were conceived in such a way that they were

---

40. the cella

felt to be incomplete in themselves; they became complete only when the building was used as a place to meet and the congregation was inside it. The architectural impulse of Dornach, in the way I've theorized it right down into the smallest details, will have a similar effect: when people enter these spaces, they'll feel drawn *to be together with other people in the space* as much as they'll be drawn to see what is performed there or to hear what is played or sung musically or recited. On the one hand, people will feel drawn to feel sympathy towards the others who have gathered there—but on the other hand they'll feel rising up within themselves the ancient question or injunction, which is as old as Western culture itself: *Know thyself!* And people will experience in the building that surrounds them something like the answer to the question: *Know thyself!* What we've attempted to do is to reproduce—artistically, not symbolically—what people can experience inwardly.

We've experienced it already: for example, whenever we've tried to recite from the space that I described to you as the organ loft, or whenever we recite or speak from the space right between the two cupolas, then the whole space takes up these things quite naturally. Every form is tailored to the word that wants to expand out within the space by way of recitation or discussion or explanation. And it's especially music that expands out within this musical-sculptural element of form that the building design at Dornach[41] is meant to represent.

With all these details, which the slides were meant to clarify to some degree, I wanted to place before your soul what the Dornach building design intends to be: a style that dissolves everything mechanical, everything geometrical, into something organic, into something that already presents the *appearance of something conscious*, so that this apparent consciousness wants to take up into itself willingly what rises up out of the depths of human consciousness.

To be sure, the result of this process is something that deviates from traditional architectural practices and norms. But anthroposophical spiritual science stands within contemporary cultural life as an ally of all the progressive forces within society, however germinal they might be, and it's staunchly opposed to all of the terribly destructive, regressive tendencies of our time. And this same progressive tendency that we're trying to nurture within anthroposophy as a teaching and a worldview is something that should be expressed through the architecture of our movement. Let that which resounds through our words in

---

41. *der Baugedanke von Dornach*

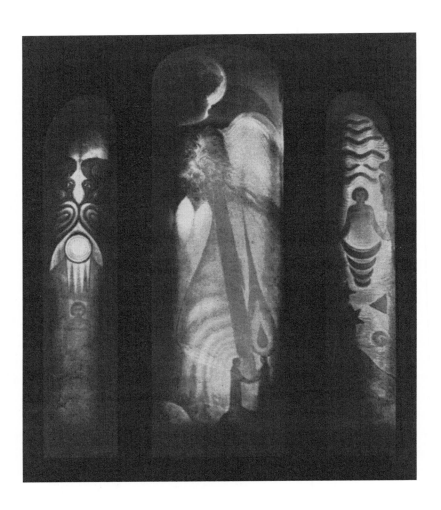

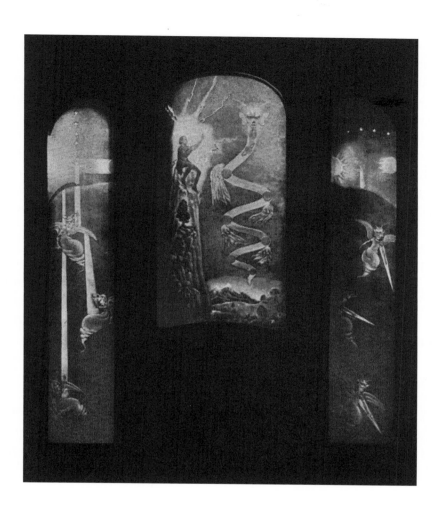

Dornach also be visible in the forms. Thus it wasn't possible for us to build in an arbitrary style; we couldn't just build any old building. Rather, the style needs to emanate from the same depths of soul and spirit that are the sources of our words. The whole architectural ideal of Dornach, the Goetheanum as a whole, is intended not as a temple, but rather a building in which people come together to receive suprasensible knowledge. Many people have described the Goetheanum as a temple, but that's just conceptual poverty speaking, an inability to find new words for new experiences. Indeed, the whole nature of the Goetheanum is antithetical to that of the old temples. Right down to the smallest details, it already conforms to something that wants to stand before the world as anthroposophy. Therefore every attempt to explain it should lead to the language and to the worldview out of which the architecture has artistically grown. And, artistically considered, I believe this building speaks for itself; it expresses its own essence and content, even if many people regard it as unjustifiable when they compare it to styles and forms that they consider the only valid formal vocabulary. Only those who have entered into anthroposophy to some degree, and have begun to comprehend its whole cultural thrust[41] will understand that a new architectural theory had to proceed from this new worldview. And even though our contemporaries may not welcome it, anthroposophy simply had to place such buildings in the world, just as it needed to speak in the way that it has. And that's why today's discussion of the Goetheanum and of the ideas underlying it can conclude with a confession of sorts: Yes, we really did try to carry out an architectural program here that was unprecedented, but it had to happen. If others hadn't dared to do such a thing at various times, there never would have been progress in the evolution of humanity. For the sake of human progress, we always have to dare to undertake something new. And even if the initial attempt is riddled with mistakes—and the person standing before you would be the first to admit it—nevertheless I have to say: such things must be attempted ever and again, as a service to humanity. And that's what we have dared to undertake over there in Dornach.

---

41. Cf. Kandinsky, *Concerning the Spiritual in Art*, p. 35: "The artist must be blind to distinctions between 'recognized' or 'unrecognized' conventions of form, deaf to the transitory teaching and demands of his particular age. He must watch only the trend of the inner need, and hearken to its words alone."

Appendix 1: Addendum to the Discussion of Slide 7*

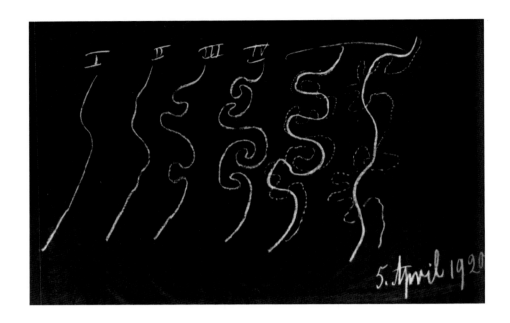

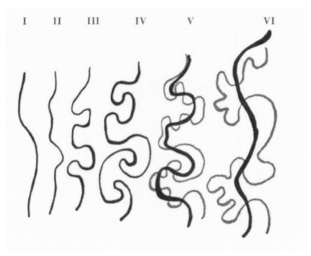

---

* This addendum is an excerpt from Steiner's lecture of April 5, 1920. The entire lecture is included in CW 288 (forthcoming).

If you follow the metamorphosis of the forces within the developmental sequence, you'll find a progression from the simple to the complex. So let me draw something simple [I]. And then the next, more complicated line might look like this [II]. Then we'd would come to a third [III], and to a fourth, which might looks something like this [IV]. Perhaps we would then have four different stages of that thing's development.

Now the next line might in some ideal sense be more complicated than the preceding form. Then we'd get this [shaded] form [V]. But this isn't what would result; rather, this other form would evolve. What I've drawn with a *thick* line would perhaps become outwardly visible then. And if we were talking about a form that really existed in nature, then we'd progress from this form to this.[†] And yet it's the case—but only within the etheric[‡]—that the development continues in such a way that the more complicated forms, which I've indicated as a shaded line, emerge, even though the physical, the outwardly visible, that which reveals itself again, simplifies itself perhaps again.

The succeeding forms might be such that the etheric forms would be these [VI, shaded]. What appears however isn't this etheric [shaded] line. Rather, what remains outwardly visible is this [*thick*] line, which represents further simplification, a substantial simplification. So if we're considering only the physical development, we rise up through a series of complications in stages I, II, III and IV, but then simplification ensues. And this really is the principle of evolution within nature herself.

---

† Presumably Steiner meant here from the line in [IV] to the simpler, thick line in [V].

‡ "The etheric" is Steiner's early term for the field of supra-physical forces that sustains life. Later he would also refer to it variously as "the life forces," or the "formative forces," or (echoing Spinoza's distinction between *natura naturans* and *natura naturata*), the realm of "living working" as opposed to the physical realm of "finished work." Theodor Schwenk's *Sensitive Chaos: The Creation of Flowing Forms in Water and Air* (London: Rudolf Steiner Press, 1996) is a scientifically compelling and aesthetically beautiful exploration of these etheric forces.

"The Faust Motif"

* Reproduced from Hilde Raske, *The Language of Color: Rudolf Steiner's Painting and Glass Windows in the First Goetheanum* (Dornach, Switzerland: Walter Keller Verlag, 1983), pp. 213-217. Raske writes of these: "The color photos reproduced here of parts of the small cupola are 'Urachromes' made by Emil Berger in 1920...when color photography was in its very beginnings. They give only a vague indication of the color values. But, because they show the conception and handling of the surfaces, it seems justified to publish them here in spite of their obvious shortcomings" (p. 213).

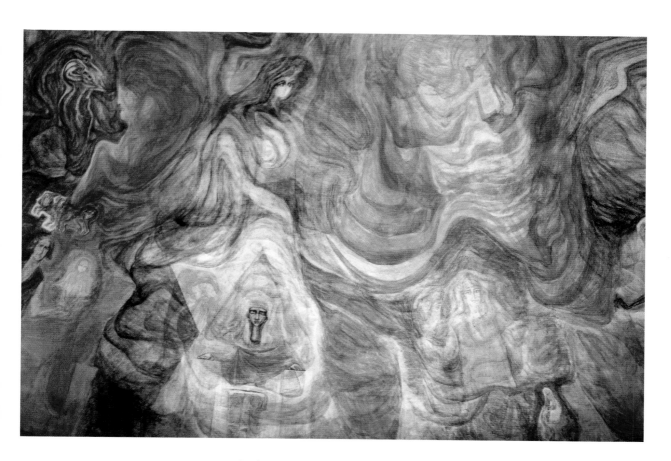

"The Greek and Egyptian Motifs"

"The Persian-Germanic and Slavic Motifs"

"The Central Motif with Blue Angel on the right and Orange Angel on the left, both with Centaur

Appendix 3: Color Drawings by van Bemmelen

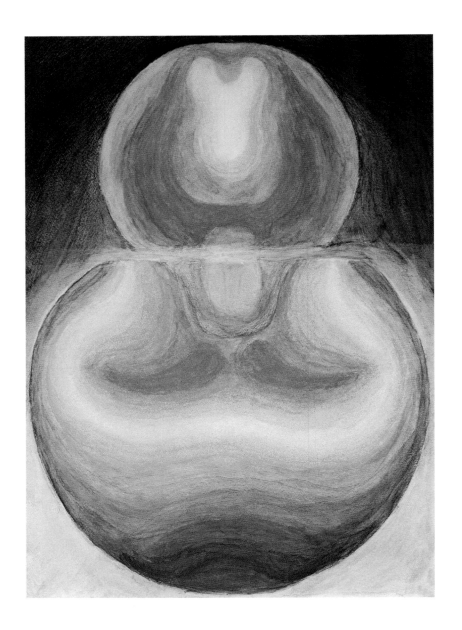

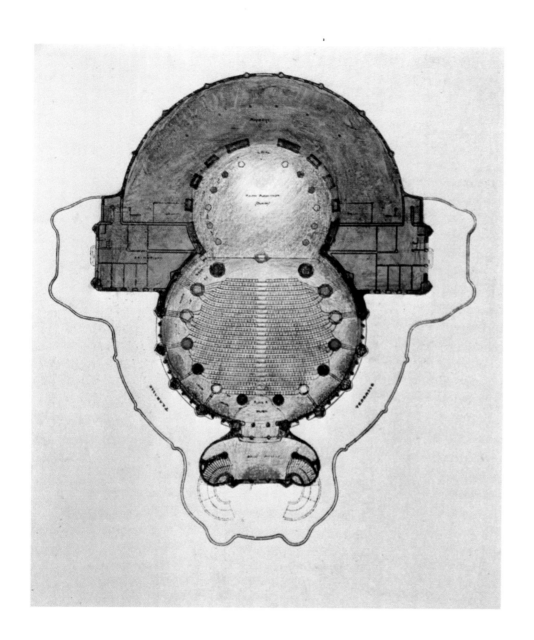

Appendix 4: Bibliographic Essay
by Frederick Amrine

The secondary literature on Rudolf Steiner as an architect and architectural theorist is already large and continues to grow. The following essay does not attempt to be comprehensive, but only to cover the most important and symptomatic publications to date, in order to help readers new to the subject orient themselves for further study.

I would like to thank Rebecca Price, the architecture historian at the University of Michigan, for her great help is assembling this bibliography.

Introductions, Biographies, and Memoirs

For a brief introduction in English to the life and work of Rudolf Steiner, see Frederick Amrine's essay "Discovering a Genius: Rudolf Steiner at 150," available online: <http://www.anthroposophy.org/fileadmin/nfm/bh-1/being-human-2011-01-Amrine-Discovering.pdf>; Robert McDermott's *The New Essential Steiner: An Introduction to Rudolf Steiner for the 21st Century* (Great Barrington, MA: Lindisfarne, 2009), 336 pp., offers a good selection of basic texts with an outstanding introduction. The standard biography of Steiner in English is now Christoph Lindenberg, *Rudolf Steiner: A Biography* (Great Barrington, MA: SteinerBooks, 2012), 816 pp., see especially Chapters 27 ("The Munich Congress: A Conference in a Rosicrucian Temple") and 33 ("Building").

Several of the artists who came to Dornach to work on the building have published reminiscences of their time there. The most important of these are by the great Russian Symbolist Andrei Bely and Assya Turgenieff, who worked on the windows. Bely's riveting memoir has been translated into German by Swetlana Geier and published under the title *Verwandeln des Lebens: Erinnerungen an Rudolf Steiner* (Basel: Zbinden Verlag, 1977), 541 pp.; see especially the chapter "Rudolf Steiner und Dornach" (pp. 314-426). Assja Turgeniev's memoir, originally in German as Assja Turgenieff, *Erinnerungen an Rudolf Steiner und die Arbeit am ersten Goetheanum* (Stuttgart: Verlag Freies

Geistesleben, 1972), has been published in English as Assya Turgenieff, *Reminiscences of Rudolf Steiner and Work on the First Goetheanum* (Forest Row: Temple Lodge, 2003), 144 pp. Another brief and very personal reminiscence of Steiner by Turgenieff has been included in the German edition of GA 287 (see below). Steiner himself published an important set of articles, "Das Goetheanum in seinen zehn Jahren," in five installments (January-March 1924) in the periodical *Das Goetheanum*; together, these also constitute a kind of memoir and reminiscence of the time when the building was under construction. They have been reprinted in GA 36, *Der Goetheanumgedanke inmitten der Kulturkrisis der Gegenwart: Gesammelte Aufsätze aus der Wochenschrift "Das Goetheanum"* (Dornach: Verlag der Rudolf Steiner-Nachlassverwaltung, 1961), pp. 305-334, but to the best of my knowledge they have not been translated into English.

Steiner's Writings on Architecture in German and English

Rudolf Steiner's lectures on architecture have been allocated to five different volumes of the *Gesamtausgabe* [GA] or *Complete Works* in German, which is published by the Rudolf Steiner Verlag in Dornach, Switzerland. These volumes have been numbered 284, 286, 287, 288, and 289/290. (The content of volume 285 has yet to be determined.) Three of these volumes were issued originally by other publishers, and two are still available in German only in editions published by other presses; presumably, these will all be reissued by the Rudolf Steiner Verlag eventually. With the publication of this volume, three have now been translated into English, and two have been integrated into the comprehensive set of *Collected Works in English* [CW] that has been undertaken by SteinerBooks.

CW 284, *Rosicrucianism Renewed: The Unity of Art, Science and Religion: The Theosophical Congress of Whitsun 1907* (Great Barrington, MA: SteinerBooks, 2007), 325 pp. + 38 plates, corresponds to GA 284, *Bilder okkulter Siegel und Säulen: Der Münchener Kongreß 1907 und seine Auswirkungen* (Dornach: Rudolf Steiner Verlag, 1997). This fine edition, a model for the whole of the CW, collects many of Steiner's addresses during the pivotal Congress of 1907 in Munich, where the seeds of all his later architectural work were planted, but also many other important texts from the years that intervened between the Congress and the building of the first Goetheanum in Dornach,

Switzerland. The volume also contains important recollections from these years by other major players in the drama, such as Marie Steiner and Karl Stockmeyer, plus translations of editor Hella Wiesberger's extensive scholarly apparatus from the German original and many colored plates.

GA 286 has been well translated by a team of five (including the anthroposophical architect Rex Raab) under the title *Architecture As a Synthesis of the Arts: Eight lectures given in Berlin and Dornach between 12 December 1911 and 26 July 1914 with an appendix featuring notes of lectures in Munich and Stuttgart on 7 and 30 March 1914, extracts from lectures in Dornach on 31 December 1923 and 1 January 1924 and two newspaper articles*, ed. and intro. Christian Thal-Jantzen (London: Rudolf Steiner Press, 1999), 192 pp. An earlier edition of the five main lectures in this volume, *Ways to a New Style in Architecture* (London: Anthroposophical Publishing Company, and New York: Anthroposophic Press, 1927), is inferior. The first German-language edition of the five central lectures in this volume (June 7, 1914-July 26, 1914) was published shortly after Steiner's death by the Philosophisch-Anthroposophischer Verlag (Dornach, 1926), and then later reissued by Verlag Freies Geistesleben (Stuttgart, 1957). A fuller version, with the additional contents included in the Rudolf Steiner Press edition, was first published by the Rudolf Steiner Verlag in 1982. Unlike any of the German originals, the English edition is graced by color reproductions, and it also offers a good brief introduction by Christian Thal-Jantzen, who likens Steiner to his contemporaries William Morris, Gaudi, and Horta. Steiner is seen as having realized the utopian architectural ideals enunciated as early as 1900 by Peter Behrens, and the editors have underscored Steiner's typically Expressionist striving to create a *Gesamtkunstwerk* by changing the title of the German original to *Architecture as a Synthesis of the Arts*. The introduction concludes with a very useful discussion of the recently completed remodeling of the interior of the second Goetheanum. The extensive notes from the German edition of 1982 (which include many important diagrams on the geometries of the first Goetheanum) have been translated meticulously.

GA 287 has been issued with the rather awkward title *Der Dornacher Bau als Wahrzeichen geschichtlichen Werdens und künstlicher Umwandlungsimpulse*, which translates literally as *The Building in Dornach as a Symbol of Historical Becoming and of Artistic Impulses for Transformation*, and would seem to have ignored Steiner's strenuous and oft-repeated protests that the Goetheanum does not contain a single symbol. The first English edition of these lectures was published by SteinerBooks in 2017 as CW 287, *Architecture as Peacework: The First Goetheanum: Dornach, 1914*. In this challenging cycle, Steiner offers an extended interpretation of the building's forms, especially the metamorphoses of the capitals and bases. He calls those forms "a script that is universal, and hence filled with meaning." The "universal meaning" that emerges is an appreciation of the unique and valuable contributions of each of the European cultures to the evolution of humanity as a whole, which Steiner offers as an overt gesture of reconciliation to counter the propaganda, hatred, and violence of World War I with actively cultivated cosmopolitanism. The first Goetheanum emerges as a powerful realization of the utopian aspirations of many Expressionist architects who were Steiner's contemporaries (see the next section of this essay below).

An English edition of GA 288, *Stilformen des Organisch-Lebendigen*, entitled *Architecture as Living Form and Organic Style* will be issued by SteinerBooks as CW 288. The six lectures allocated to GA 288 were originally published in well-edited editions by the Philosophisch-Anthroposophischer Verlag between 1933 and 1942. Here Steiner seeks to situate his own work within the history of architecture. He recounts how he had witnessed the remarkable architectural transformation of Vienna in the second half of the nineteenth century, and that he had studied under Gottfried Semper's student Heinrich von Ferstel at the *Technische Hochschule*. Steiner calls for a new kind of spiritual organicism that sorts very well with the better-known Expressionist manifestos of Steiner's student, Wassily Kandinsky, for example. Reflecting on the differences between sculpting in marble and in wood, Steiner shows an appreciation of the intimate relationship between form and material that anticipates the Bauhaus. Like Goethe, Steiner claims that art is cognitive; that it reveals hidden forces that nature would not have revealed otherwise. But he calls for a deeply organic style that would represent a new Goetheanism, rather than that of 1832 (the year of Goethe's death).

CW 289 will include ten lectures intended for eventual publication as GA 289, three of which were pre-issued as *Architektur, Plastik, und Malerei des Ersten Goetheanum: Drei Vorträge gehalten in Dornach am 23., 24. und 25. Januar 1920.*

CW 290 is the present volume, which corresponds to GA 290; *Der Baugedanke des Goetheanum: Einleitender Vortrag mit Erklärungen zu den Bildern des*

Goetheanum-Baues gehalten in Bern am 29. Juni 1921. It was first published by Philosophisch-Anthroposophischer Verlag, Dornach, in 1932. A special edition of this lecture, with a lavish array of photographs in black-and-white and color, appeared as *Das Goetheanum als Gesamtkunstwerk: Der Baugedanke des Goetheanum* (Dornach: Philosophisch-Anthroposophischer Verlag, 1986), 286 pp.

Andrew Beard has edited a useful selection of texts by Steiner on architecture, Rudolf Steiner, *Architecture: An Introductory Reader*, ed. and intro. Andrew Beard (Forest Row: Sophia Books, 2003), 274 pp. Most, but not all, of these lectures and excerpts had previously been published elsewhere. One exception is Chapter 8, which is particularly germane because it offers an "edited version" of a slide lecture on the first Goetheanum, very similar to the one contained in this volume, given by Rudolf Steiner in the Hague earlier the same year (February 28, 1921). The German original of this lecture has not been published as part of the *Gesamtausgabe*, and the source has been identified only as a "typescript," so it is not clear what kind of editing has been done. Beard's chapters are organized by theme, and they give the reader tastes from a broader range of Steiner's writings than the aforementioned five volumes of the GA. Seven of this collection's twelve chapters reprint texts that are contained in *Architecture as a Synthesis of the Arts*. There are five excerpts from *Art in the Light of Mystery Wisdom*, plus a smattering of passages from various other lecture cycles such as *Universe, Earth and Man* and *Occult Signs and Symbols*. The last sections invite us to view Steiner's architecture against the backdrop of The Temple Legend. Part of Steiner's dedication of the Stuttgart House, on October 15, 1911, is included (the full version of which is available in English in CW 284). All previously issued translations were revised for this volume by Matthew Barton. Andrew Beard's succinct introduction both situates Steiner within the history of architecture and suggests important esoteric dimensions of his architectural theories.

Rudolf Steiner as an Architect

The seminal article contributed by Kenneth Bayes to A. C. Harwood's now-classic volume *The Faithful Thinker* (London: Hodder and Stoughton, 1961, pp. 163-178), "Architecture in Accord with Man," can be identified, I believe, as the turning-point in the scholarly reception of Steiner's architecture.[*] Bayes is quoted extensively in Dennis Sharp's early study *Modern Architecture and Expressionism* (1966), which seems in turn to have been the primary influence on Wolfgang Pehnt's still-definitive study *Expressionist Architecture* (1973). Hence Bayes can be viewed as the patriarch of mainstream scholarship on Steiner as an architect, and for that reason he deserves mention here, even though his essay is more about Steiner's place within the history of architecture than Steiner's buildings themselves. Bayes's argument is both sophisticated and prophetic: he situates Steiner firmly within a succession of architectural "odd men out" that seemed to have been rendered irrelevant by Modernism (Ruskin and Morris, van de Velde, Horta, Häring, Poelzig, Mendelsohn), only to experience a revival in the postwar years. For Bayes, the revival of that neglected stream proves that there were "two starters" in the history of twentieth-century architecture, rather than just one. Indeed, it is easy to make the case that developments in architecture since 1961 have turned the tables, and a program that we might want to label "Expressionist" (although Bayes himself does not employ the term) now seems to have been the mainstream, with Modernism as an exceptional interlude. Bayes also notes in this early study an architectural conception that he believes is "unique to Steiner": the idea that architecture should "be formed by cosmic space around it, by the forces pouring in from the periphery" (p. 174). This idea of "counter-space" [*Gegenraum*], as George Adams terms it in his seminal essay included in the same volume, is best captured in terms of projective geometry. Many anthroposophical scientists have taken up Steiner's advice to explore this "qualitative geometry" more fully,[†] but scholars have barely begun to study this aspect of Steiner's architecture, no doubt because, as Bayes himself allows, it is a highly esoteric idea that is "difficult to put in words" (p. 175).

Erich Zimmer's handsome, large format volume *Rudolf Steiner als Architekt von Wohn- und Zweckbauten* (Stuttgart: Verlag Freies Geistesleben, 1971), 246 pp., which covers all of Steiner's buildings *except* the first and second Goetheanum, is still one of the finest studies of Steiner's architecture available. The selection of photos and drawings is rich and well chosen, and there is also a

---

[*] But see also my discussion of the remarkable four-part essay of 1960 by Mario Brunati and Sandro Mendini, discussed below.
[†] See the many important publications by George Adams, Louis Locher-Ernst, Olive Whicher, and Lawrence Edwards, among others.

comprehensive list of Steiner's extant models and sketches on pp. 244-245. Zimmer describes each building in meticulous detail, but he also enters deeply into the underlying architectural theories. This volume really deserves to be translated into English.

Eloquent Concrete: How Rudolf Steiner Employed Reinforced Concrete (London: Rudolf Steiner Press, 1979), 180 pp., by Rex Raab, Arne Klingborg and Åke Fant was originally published in German under the title *Sprechender Beton: Wie Rudolf Steiner den Stahlbeton verwendete* (Dornach: Philosophisch-Anthroposophischer Verlag, 1972). The central focus of this important study is the second Goetheanum, but it also covers the Heating Plant, Haus Duldeck, the Haus de Jaager, and the Eurythmeum. There is a set of very instructive overlays (both floor plan and longitudinal section) that allow one to see immediately the proportions of the first compared to the second Goetheanum. An extensive bibliography includes many references that could not be included here. The most valuable aspect of this volume is arguably the first chapter, "Modern Architects Make a Discovery," in which the authors describe recent discussions of Steiner by major architects and architectural historians. They recount the meeting in which Hans Scharoun (who designed the Berlin Philharmonic) declared the second Goetheanum to be "the most significant building of the first half of the century," and they also summarize several publications on Steiner and Gaudi by the important Japanese architect Kenji Imai.

Another study that appeared in 1972 was Eugene A. Santomasso's Columbia University dissertation, *Origins and Aims of German Expressionist Architecture: An Essay into the Expressionist Frame of Mind in Germany, Especially as Typified in the Work of Rudolf Steiner*. He sees four main ideals associated with Expressionism: "(1) that of fostering a new architecture inspired by both traditional building forms and by organic and inorganic forms of nature, (2) of employing various materials and forms so as to elicit one's empathetic involvement with the building (the aesthetics of *Einfühlung*), (3) of controlling and augmenting the effects of empathetic formal expression through a synthesis of diverse artistic media and sensory effects (the ideal of the *Gesamtkunstwerk*), and (4) the utopian ideal of creating an architecture that is both at one with and demonstrative of spiritual forces in the cosmos." His coverage of Steiner, however, is slender and weak; rather his focus is on extra-architectural matters.

In his fine essay of 1975, ("Architecture: Buildings for Life," in *Work Arising from the Life of Rudolf Steiner* [London: Rudolf Steiner Press, 1975], pp. 61-76), Rex Raab describes the first Goetheanum as a "spiritual workshop … where knowledge, art and social life could be woven together in a heightened form" (p. 63). This has since given rise to a large architectural movement. "A central architectural question contained in all these projects is that of the relation between form and function"; anthroposophical architects seek "an 'organic' solution" and "a living form." They "become aware … that certain habits of thought … must now be metamorphosed if progress is to be made and freedom reached" (p. 70). "The new architectural image-building power is able, systematically trained, to become 'exact phantasy,' a precise instrument in the hands of the moulding and shaping architect and designer. Only the individual so equipped will be able to work in the true interests of the community" (p. 73).

Another fine early recognition of Steiner's importance as an architect is Vittorio Leti Messina's *L'Architetture della libertà: Studi sul pensiero architettonico di Rudolf Steiner* (L'Aquila: L. U. Japadre Editore, 1976). Writing as a practicing architect rather than a historian, Messina attempts to counter what he sees as reflexive dismissals of Steiner, and his book is more specifically a systematic response to a critical article by the eminent historian Bruno Zevi that had been published in 1975 (*L'Espresso*, No. 12, March). Steiner's architecture is situated within the larger context of Steiner's unconventional thinking about space, time, and mathematics, which yielded unique notions of architectural language and discourse. It follows from Steiner's "philosophy of freedom" that he broke with all inherited forms to create an "architecture of freedom," and hence Messina argues that it makes little sense to criticize Steiner as idiosyncratic. The main influence on Steiner's architectural thinking lay entirely outside the mainstream: Goethe's scientific work and its implicit epistemology, which Steiner had worked out in the process of editing those works for the critical "Weimar" edition. Goethe led Steiner to create a new kind of organic architecture that was both dynamic and highly expressive. Especially interesting are Messina's accounts of Steiner's influence on Mendelsohn and Wright[*] and his concluding chapter, "Prolegomeni ad una architettura della libertà." The format of the book is small, and the selection of photos and diagrams at the end of the volume is minimal, so newcomers will want to supplement

---

[*] See John Kettle's introduction to the present volume.

their reading of Messina by consulting other studies with better illustrations. Messina seems to have won over Bruno Zevi eventually, however, since Zevi later included Messina's book *Rudolf Steiner architetto* (Torino: Testo & Immagine, 1996) as volume 11 in his series *Universale di Architettura*. Although the format is again small, this later volume is lavishly illustrated in both black-and-white and color. Here many of the key points from the earlier study are recapitualated briefly, but the emphasis is more biographical and historical than philosophical. Messina concludes this introduction to Steiner with a very useful overview of subsequent architects who have self-identified as "anthroposophical," including several who have become important architects in their own right (e.g. Alberts and Van Huut, Imre Macovecz, Kenji Imai, Erik Asmussen). Guy Rumé's essay "Rudolf Steiner" (*Architecture, mouvement, continuité*, 39 [June 1976], 23-29 is less successful in its attempts to understand Steiner's architectural impulse.

A classic study originally in German, and perhaps the best introduction to the topic from an unapologetically anthroposophical perspective, is Hagen Biesantz and Arne Klingborg's *Das Goetheanum: Der Bau-Impuls Rudolf Steiners* (Dornach: Philosophisch-Anthroposophischer Verlag, 1978), 130 pp., which has been issued in English as *The Goetheanum: Rudolf Steiner's Architectural Impulse* (London: Rudolf Steiner Press, 1979), 132 pp. The final chapters offer a solid, concise account of Steiner's subsequent influence, including a long list of anthroposophical architects with biographical dates, the names and locations of buildings, and some photos (pp. 111-123). Hagen Biesantz has contributed the main body of the book, which consists of extended essays on the first Goetheanum and the second Goetheanum, plus a shorter narrative about the roots of anthroposophical architecture in Munich and Stuttgart between 1907 and September 20, 1913, when the foundation stone of the first Goetheanum was laid. Biesantz has also graced the volume with a penetrating, concise statement of the main principles of Steiner's aesthetics more generally, on pp. 83-89.

Another important contribution to our understanding of Steiner's architecture that might easily be overlooked is the paperback issued by DuMont in 1980, *Rudolf Steiner und seine Architektur*. Edited by Mike Schuyt and Joost Elffers, with an accompanying text by Peter Ferger, this slender volume is profusely illustrated, ambitious, dense, and philosophical verging on meditative. Ferger insists on Steiner's uniqueness, and he explicitly rejects comparisons with historical architectural styles such as Expressionism or Art Nouveau because Steiner was neither an architect in the conventional sense nor do his works constitute an architectural "oeuvre." On this account, Steiner's architecture is a completely new impulse, an immediate expression of direct spiritual experience that can be understood only within the context of Steiner's unique epistemology, aesthetics, and spiritual psychology. Out of these fundamental insights arose the qualities and principles that animate Steiner's buildings, such as metamorphosis, an "appearance of consciousness," transparency, vitalism, and the intention to effect moral transformation in the viewer. Aside from careful descriptions of Steiner's buildings (and the many accompanying photos), there is little outside of anthroposophy itself to help orient newcomers, who may find this uncompromising introduction surprisingly challenging.

Rex Raab's "Rudolf Steiner as an Architect," in *Architectural Association Quarterly*, 12.3 (1980), pp. 48-55, gives a loose overview of his work, then calls for "a continuation of the sober and consistent examination of Rudolf Steiner's contribution to architectural thinking and practice, as exemplified in the writings of distinguished critics such as Dennis Sharp, Wolfgang Pehnt and Kenji Imai" (p. 54). Secondarily, he "would appeal for an organic approach to architecture, such as has been preparing in the womb of time" (p. 54). "Steiner's architectural impulse is this: not to supply us with ready-made solutions, but to encourage each one of us to find himself as an architect; to find the higher human being in himself and his client; to tap the source of architectural imagination that slumbers in every man" (p. 55).

Wolfgang Bachmann's *Die Architekurvorstellungen der Anthroposophen: Versuch einer Deutung und Wertung* (Köln/Wien: Böhlau Verlag, 1981), originally a dissertation at the TH Aachen, makes no pretense to scholarly objectivity; it is more like journalism. Name-calling takes the place of scholarly analysis. Steiner's worldview underlies it, and it's exotic! Bachmann went looking for sectarianism, and he found it. He makes no attempt to gain a balanced and objective picture.

Martin Filler's "Fantasms and Fragments: Expressionist Architecture" (*Art in Architecture*, January 1983) contains only a paragraph on Steiner, and it's very strange. The second Goetheanum is said to resemble a bust of Darth Vader (!), then dismissed as only "a marginal curiosity, superficially Expressionist is style while remaining, under its forcefully modeled exterior, basically as modern as the Wagner Festspielhaus at Bayreuth" (p. 113). A much more sophisticated account of Steiner's architecture, especially his debt to Goethe, is Christa Lichtenberg's treatment of Rudolf Steiner in volume one of a two-volume work, *Die Wirkungsgeschichte der Metamorphosenlehre Goethes: Von Philipp Otto Runge bis Joseph Beuys* (Weinheim: VCH Verlagsgesellschaft, 1990), pp. 69-79. Her comparison of Steiner's wielding of sculptural forms with Brancusi and other cubists is especially intriguing.

Hans-Jürgen Schleicher's *Architektur als Welterfahrung: Rudolf Steiners organischer Baustil und die Architektur der Waldorfschulen* (Frankfurt am Main: Fischer Taschenbuch Verlag, 1987) is divided into two parts. The first is a more general introduction to architecture as such; the second is devoted more to the needs of the Waldorf School movement. As a result of Steiner's intensive preoccupation with Goethe's worldview, he developed a unique theory of organic form, and a deep feeling for gesture. The school is viewed as part of the natural environment, of the cultural environment, and of the social processes in which it is embedded. The book concludes with an appendix on organic building.

Rudolf Steiner: Goetheanum, Dornach by the eminent architectural historian Wolfgang Pehnt (Ernst & Sohn, 1991), 95 pp., is an outstanding bilingual introduction to Rudolf Steiner as an architect, with English facing the German original. The color photographs of Steiner's major buildings (all but the first Goetheanum, alas) are the best available in print by far. It speaks to Steiner's importance as an architect that the *doyen* of the architectural history of Expressionism decided he merited a full study. The text is concise, brimming with facts, insightful, and respectful without being adulatory. As one might expect, Pehnt has the most to say about Steiner as an Expressionist, both his relationship to others within the same movement and the many ways in which he realized their utopian ideals by creating multiple genuine *Gesamtkunstwerke*. Pehnt also offers many insights into relationships among the many buildings that together make up Dornach as an integral architectural site.

Sonja Marion Brigitta Ohlenschläger's doctoral dissertation, *Die Architekturen Rudolf Steiners* (Bonn, 1992), 359 pp., is a solid, general study, which begins with Steiner's biography and a chapter recounting the main ideas of anthroposophical aesthetics, then proceeds to narrate the history of Steiner's architectural efforts from the Munich Congress of 1907 through the second Goetheanum. Special attention is given to the concepts of metamorphosis and *Umstülpung* [turning-inside-out]. Dornach is considered as a "colony," and compared to Monte Verità. One chapter poses the question: Is the Goetheanum a temple? Steiner's work is situated within other interpretive contexts: organicism, the *Gesamtkunstwerk*, parallels with Fidus, Scharoun, and Hugo Häring.

Paulgerd Jesberg has a number of important studies in the October 1992 edition of the *Bauzeitschrift* (40.2) which is devoted to the topic of organic building. Two main articles are devoted to "Organisches Bauen" (pp. 1813-1816) and "Goetheanum und das Bauen heute" (pp. 1831-1838), but there is also extensive coverage of anthroposophical architecture throughout the issue: "Nichts: Organische Städtebau" (pp.1757-1760); "Steinerschule in Stavanger/N" (pp. 1779-1784); "Sekem Farm in Ägypten" (pp. 1785-1790); "Festsaal in Järna/SF" (pp. 1791-1796); "Naturata in Überlingen" (pp. 1797-1804); and "Altenwohnanlage in Birkach" (pp. 1805-1810).

Beat Wyss's book *Der Wille zur Kunst: Zur ästhetischen Mentalität der Moderne* (Köln: Dumont, 1996) devotes a section (pp. 142-157) to Steiner. In it, Wyss reads the forms of the first Goetheaum's bases and capitals as a systematic transposition of Goethe's poem (not the treatise) *The Metamorphosis of Plants*. Less persuasive is his claim that the cupola represents a great skull.

David Adams' fine study "The Goetheanum as White Magic, or Why Is Anthroposophical Architecture So Important?" (*Journal for Anthroposphy*, 64 [Spring 1997], pp. 13-46, relates "some of the most esoteric spiritual reasons why Steiner attached such importance to his architectural work and why to the Goetheanum in particular" (p. 16). Steiner consciously intended his architecture to "*help* humanity conquer materialism, properly prepare the future, feel itself expanded into the spiritual cosmos, and spiritually bring the life of feeling into balance and order" (p. 19). The result is nothing short of white magic.

Anna Sokolina's Russian-language study of 2001, Архитектура и Антропософия [*Anthroposophy and Architecture*] (n.p.: Издательство КМК), is very fine. It collects articles by Franz Carlgren, Åke Fant, Wolfgang Pehnt, Hagen Biesantz, Rex Raab, Arne Klingborg, Georg Hartmann, Christian Kisch, Erik Asmussen, Jens Peters, among others. The volume concludes with a brief essay by Sokolina, usefully in English: although brief, it is excellent, especially on the anthroposophical architects Erik Asmussen and Imre Makovecz.

Another more recent general study is Werner Blaser's handsome bilingual edition *Natur im Gebauten: Nature in Building: Rudolf Steiner in Dornach* (Basel: Birkhäuser, 2002), 128 pp. Blaser, who studied with Alvar Aalto and

Mies van der Rohe, offers a crisp, profusely illustrated introduction to the architecture of the anthroposophical community in Dornach as a whole as it exists today. (There is only a brief discussion of the first Goetheanum.)

Walter Kugler and Simon Baur's *Rudolf Steiner in Kunst und Architektur* (Köln: Dumont Buchverlag, 2007) is an excellent collection, which reprints many of the best pieces on Steiner's aesthetics generally and architecture specifically. Important pieces by Sharp (1966), Pehnt (1994), Oberhuber (1995), Lichtenstern (1990), Wyss (1996), and Rotzler (1960) are all discussed elsewhere in this bibliographic essay.

Pieter van der Ree's attractive book, *Formen schaffen als Ausdruck inneren Erlebens: Rudolf Steiners Kunst und Architektur als Bild des inneren Schulungsweges* (Stuttart: Verlag Freies Geistesleben, 2009), places Steiner's architecture against the background of esoteric development, beginning with the rose cross meditation, and moving to the important impulses arising out of the Munich Congress of 1907. He sees the first Goetheanum as the inner path made visible, the first and second Goetheanum as an image of the human being, and both buildings as a union of microcosm and macrocosm. It is an excellent study, esoteric yet clear.

Espen Tharaldsen's *Die Verwandlung des Alltags: Rudolf Steiners Ästhetik* (Stuttgart: Verlag Freies Geistesleben, 2012) unfolds as an imaginary conversation between Hjalmar and Charlotte. It is more about Steiner's general aesthetics, indeed about Steiner generally, than about architecture specifically, but there are some nice observations towards the end of the volume about Steiner's functionalism.

Surely the most important recent study that is available in English is the comprehensive catalogue of the exhibition *Rudolf Steiner: Alchemy of the Everyday* at the Vitra Design Museum (2013) in Weil, Germany, near Basel. This beautifully produced, profusely illustrated catalogue covers not only Steiner's architecture, but also other aspects of his work as a visual artist, including extensive discussion of anthroposophical furniture design. The volume opens with Walter Kugler's precise and evocative general introduction to Steiner as a thinker (pp. 24-37), and it continues with a wealth of outstanding contributions, including yet another succinct overview of Steiner's architecture by Wolfgang Pehnt.[*] Kugler situates Steiner within a broad intellectual-historical

---

[*] pp. 108-119. See the discussion of his recent book devoted entirely to Steiner above, and of his seminal study *Expressionist Architecture* below.

context that includes other modern thinkers and artists such as Haeckel, the "philosopher of the unconscious" von Hartmann, Klee, Holz, Rilke, and even Borges. In "Goetheanum Style and Aesthetic Individualism" (pp. 132-142), Reinhold J. Fäth provides a useful overview of Steiner's aesthetics, which he organizes under the rubrics "Individualism," "Art as Spiritual Activity," "The Aura of the Manufacturing Process," "Colour," "The Inclining Gesture," "The Organic Principle," "Living Surfaces," "The Upper End," and "Visible Music." The other especially noteworthy contribution is Pieter van der Ree's essay "Living Thought and Plastic Art" (pp. 184-194), which seeks to situate Steiner's organicism within the history of twentieth-century art and architecture.

The First Goetheanum

Carl Kemper (1881-1957) was a sculptor who came to Dornach in 1914, helped to carve the first Goetheanum, and then became a scholar of the building. After his death, five colleagues (Hilde Raske, Albert von Baravalle, Friedrich Häusler, Heinrich Kern, and Georg Unger) together edited Kemper's many manuscripts and published them posthumously in Carl Kemper, *Der Bau: Studien zur Architektur und Plastik des Ersten Goetheanum* [*The Building: Studies on the Architecture and Sculpture of the First Goetheanum*], ed. Hilde Raske (Stuttgart: Verlag Freies Geistesleben, 1966; 2nd edn. 1974), 272 pp. This early collection of materials is still arguably the most fundamentally thorough study of the first Goetheanum, presenting and describing many drawings, models, and lecture notes pertaining to the original construction. Topics that are covered in depth include the concept of metamorphosis and the mathematical structure of the building, which Kemper sought to understand principally in terms of non-Euclidean or "qualitative" geometry. Georg Unger's presentation of the latter is especially penetrating. Hilde Raske's chapter "Language of Forms" covers the motifs of the columns, capitals, architraves, and bases. Kemper also closely studied Steiner's planetary seals as examples of metamorphic inversion. Heinrich Kern covers the work that relates Steiner to Goethe, and also the morphology of Steiner's architecture as compared with the anatomy of the human body, a topic that Steiner addresses in many different contexts (notably in his cycle of lectures on astronomy in its relationship to the other scientific disciplines [GA 323]). The volume also features discussions of the building's plans and proportions by the architect von Baravalle, and a short biography of Kemper by Hilde Raske.

Daniel van Bemmelen's *Das erste Goetheanum als Menschheitsbau* (Dornach: Philosophisch-Anthroposophischer Verlag, 1975), 94 pp., is an older study that remains unavailable in English. This highly esoteric booklet is divided into two chapters: "The First Goetheanum as a Temple of the Human Body" and "The First Goetheanum as the House of Anthroposophia." The former covers Agrippa von Nettesheim's six archetypal human poses, Egyptian myth, and the sacred geometries of ancient temples, especially the Temple of Solomon. The second is devoted primarily to the program of the stained glass windows as relating to the stages of higher development.

Erich Zimmer's fine study *Der Modellbau von Malsch und das Erste Goetheanum* (Stuttgart: Verlag Freies Geistesleben, 1979) is short and very esoteric. Indeed, it was originally a private publication. He traces with great subtlety the ways in which the eliptical, temple-like model of a building in Malsch gave way to the more elaborate, theatrical space of the first Goetheanum. The important constant underlying both buildings is the Goethean theory of metamorphosis.

Hilde Raske is herself the author of another major study that fortunately has been translated into English: *The Language of Color in the First Goetheanum: A Study of Rudolf Steiner's Art* (Dornach: Walter Keller Verlag, 1982), 288 pp. The German original was published by Verlag Freies Geistesleben in 1983 under the title *Das Farbenwort*. This insightful study, devoted entirely to the paintings on the ceilings of the two cupolas of the first Goetheanum, is profusely illustrated in black-and-white and color (including Emil Berger's early color "Urachromes" appended to the present volume).

Konrad Oberhuber's major study "Rudolf Steiner – Das Erste Goetheaum," in the volume *Okkultismus und Avantgarde: Von Munch bis Mondrian 1900-1915* (Ostfildern: Edition Tertium, 1915, pp. 712-757), is lavishly illustrated, with 21 black-and-white and 38 colored plates. He reads the building as a series of polarities: bearing and loading; cloaking and radiation; convex and concave; warm and cold; light and dark; systole and diastole. The stage is the "older" space, a Euclidean circle; the audience is a "new" space, built up through tangential rays in a non-Euclidean fashion. He discerns a threefold pattern in the building's structure: the zone of the bases (body), the windows and wall (soul), and the cupola (spirit). In the middle realm, the realm of the soul, the building is most alive: "In the zone of the wall, on the other hand, the actual polarity of bearing and loading, of concave and convex, light and shadow, and therewith of inhalation and exhalation, of systole and diastole, unfolds. Here is the zone of organic life and thus of the transformations, of the metamorphoses, when the forms transform themselves in accord with their functions. Here the building communicates through the light with the world. It breathes together with the environment."

The Second Goetheanum

An early "mainstream" study of the second Goetheanum by Willy Roetzler, "Das Goetheanum in Dornach als Beispiel der Integration der Künste" (*Werk*, No. 8, August 1960, pp. 281-285) is indicative of the difficulties scholars outside of anthroposophical circles have had in trying to come to terms with Steiner's buildings. This brief but dense and well-illustrated article begins by rightly viewing Steiner within the general modernist striving to integrate all the arts into a *Gesamtkunstwerk*, but he wrongly attributes Steiner's success to the building's supposed purpose as the focal point of a "cult." Confusingly, he declares it to be both derivative of Art Nouveau and a "special case within expressionism" (p. 283). Roetzler does considerably better in an aside on the first Goetheanum, in which he notes echoes of early Christian domed churches in Syria, speculates about the possible influence of the Swiss sculptor Hermann Obrist (1863-1927, an exact contemporary of Steiner who was, like Steiner, working in Munich), and finally declares the building to have been a single, monolithic Expressionist sculpture. Returning to the second Goethean towards the end of his article, Roetzler finally loses his scholarly composure, labeling the building "ponderous," "irrational," and "bunker-like." He describes its appearance colorfully as "schwerblütig-dumpf," an untranslatable neologism that means something like "ham-handed." He declares it *sui generis*—and then holds it up as a singularly successful realization of the ideal of the *Gesamtkunstwerk*.

Georg Hartmann's *Goetheanum Glasfenster* (Dornach: Philosophisch-Anthroposophischer Verlag, 1971, 2nd edn. 1983), 75pp., is an introduction to the glass windows in the second Goetheanum. It includes numerous plates both in black-and-white and in color.

A series of illustrated articles on artistic questions connected with the translation of Steiner's designs for elements from the interior of the first

Goetheanum into an appropriate expression for the interior of the second Goetheanum is available as "The Great Hall of the Goetheanum—Its Completion at the End of the Century," Special English Edition of *Stil* magazine, Arts Section of the School of Spiritual Science, 1994 (available from Art Section, c/o Christian Thal-Jantzen, Mulberry House, 16 Hoathly Hill, West Hoathly, West Sussex, RH19 4SJ.)

Erika von Baravalle's "Der Michaelsbau: Zum Raumgedanken des Zweiten Goetheaum," in her book *Rudolf Steiners Grundsteinlegung am 20. September 1913 im Angesicht der Sterne* (Arlesheim: Verlag des Ita Wegman Instituts, 2013) sees the second Goetheaum in light of a comment by Ita Wegman of May 3, 1925. Wegman saw it as a "Michaelic fortress," together with the karma lectures of 1924 and the First Class, one of three great deeds flowing from the Christmas Conference.

Jonathan Alesander's *Imagining the Goetheanum: An Architectural Exploration in the Language of Polar Logic* (n.p.: Polar Press, 2015) is a non-scholarly book that is however excellent. He covers many features that have been treated in greater depth elsewhere. A somewhat odd feature is the introduction of Coleridge's polar logic as an explanatory category. Especially fine is the phenomenological treatment of the umbra morphology—the changing play of light and shadow—upon the various faces of the building.

Rudolf Steiner's Place in the History of Architecture

In many ways, the reception of Steiner's work mirrors the reception of architectural Expressionism as a movement: neglect followed by the growing realization that what had seemed at best a fleeting episode at the margins turns out to have been the first chapter of a central narrative. Only in light of later work by architects such as Scharoun, Gehry, Cardinal, Le Corbusier, Saarinen, and Wright —not to mention the many architects who self-identify as anthroposophists or were directly inspired by Steiner—did the import of Steiner and the other Expressionists finally become visible.

Given that Hans Scharoun declared the second Goetheanum to be the most significant building of the first half of the twentieth century,[*] and that it had such a profound influence on both Le Corbusier and Frank Lloyd Wright,[†]

---

[*] Quoted e.g. in the initial chapter of Rex Raab et al., *Eloquent Concrete*.
[†] See John Kettle's account in the introduction to the present volume.

it is hard to imagine Steiner not rating even a mention in a major work of architectural history. Yet several major studies ignore him completely. That is the case in Sigfried Giedion's classic study *Space, Time and Architecture: the growth of a new tradition* (5th edn., Cambridge: Harvard UP, 1980), based on his Charles Eliot Norton Lectures delivered at Harvard University in 1938-1939. And Giedion barely touches on Expressionism as a movement, granting it only two pages out of 897! Worse, the little that Giedion has to say about Expressionism is cursory and condescending: "Faustian outbursts against an inimical world and the cries of outraged humanity cannot create new levels of achievement. They remain transitory facts—however moving they may be—and not constituent ones. The Expressionist influence could not perform any service for architecture. Nevertheless it touched almost every German worker in the arts. Men who were later to do grimly serious work in housing developments abandoned themselves to romantic mysticism, dreamed of fairy castles to stand on the peak of Monte Rosa. Others built concrete towers as flaccid as jellyfish" (p. 486).

Giedion's study is symptomatic of the degree to which architectural Expressionism has been actively ignored by historians for decades. The eminent historian of architecture Charles Jencks has noted and discussed this issue in his book *Modern Movements in Architecture* (Garden City, NY: Doubleday, 1973). In his introduction Jencks laments that recent historians of architecture have "implicitly [become] either an apologist for a single tradition, say the International Style, or the prophet of inevitable development, say technology and structural determinism…and so the amount of live traditions or alternatives to the future is radically limited. Because of such suppression two architectural movements, Futurism and Expressionism, were surgically removed from our memory for thirty years" (pp. 12-13). Yet Jencks fails to correct for the bias in his own book! It contains no chapter on Expressionism (which he subsumes within a "tradition" he calls "intuitive"), and it makes no mention whatsoever of Rudolf Steiner, even though Dennis Sharp's important study (see below) had been available since 1966. An even greater omission is his unwillingness to identify important late twentieth-century buildings as "Expressionist"—not even Hans Scharoun's Philharmonic Hall in Berlin, despite Scharoun having been a card-carrying Expressionist as a young man. Instead, Jencks categorizes them under the derogatory term "fantastic." And in 1999, Jencks was willing to devote only forty words to Steiner—right after implying that anthroposophy is "more solid ground" than Einstein's General Theory of Relativity, which Erich Mendelsohn's Einstein Tower had sought to incarnate! But even at this late date, his book *Ecstatic Architecture: The Surprising Link* (Chichester: Academy Editions, 1999) still refuses to call either Mendelsohn or Steiner by their proper names, Expressionist.

Other important histories of architecture in which Steiner is not mentioned at all include John Peter's *Masters of Modern Architecture* (New York: George Braziller, 1958), Leonardo Benevolo's *History of Modern Architecture*, 2 vols. (Cambridge, MA: MIT Press, 1971),* and Kenneth Frampton's *Modern Architecture: A Critical History* (London: Thames and Hudson, 1985). Benevolo also makes no mention of Expressionism, subsuming anything that might have been properly identified as such under the rubric "Art Nouveau." Peter Gössel's and Gabriele Leuthäuser's *Architecture in the Twentieth Century* (Köln: Benedikt Taschen Verlag, 1991) is another attempt at a comprehensive history that fails to mention Steiner; inexplicably, the second Goetheanum is ignored even in a chapter entitled "Creative in Concrete." Another important book which many consider definitive, Spiro Kostof's *A History of Architecture: Settings and Rituals* (New York: Oxford UP, 1995), likewise overlooks Steiner completely.

Although it was edited by Wolfgang Pehnt, who would later publish extensively on Expressionist architecture generally and Rudolf Steiner specifically, the *Encyclopedia of Modern Architecture* (New York: Abrams, 1964) devotes no entry to Steiner. However, the second Goetheanum is mentioned very briefly in the article on Expressionism: "Rudolf Steiner's Goetheanum at Dornach (1925-8) is linked to Expressionism by its picturesque treatment, but occupies a place apart, as it was designed in accordance with the principles of Anthroposophy" (p. 96). It is hard to imagine what the author of this entry might have meant by "picturesque," and it is hard to understand how this lazy dismissal was allowed to stand by an editor of Pehnt's stature. It would take another decade before Wolfgang Pehnt himself was finally able to give Steiner and Expressionism the scholarly respect they deserve (see below).

Henry-Russell Hitchcock's widely read history, *Architecture: Nineteenth and Twentieth Centuries* (Harmondsworth: Penguin, 1971), segues from an odd discussion of Mendelsohn's Einstein Tower as an example of "mechanistic" organicism to a single, brief mention of Steiner and a mischaracterization of

---

* The omission is not merely a matter of translation, as the Italian original is similarly lacking.

his masterpiece: "The extreme point of this sort of abstract sculptural Expressionism in the twenties is found in the executed work of no architect but in the cult edifice called Goetheanum at Dornach in Switzerland, designed by the creator of anthroposophy Rudolf Steiner and begun in 1923."

Two other important histories reveal just how hard it is for architectural historians to respect Steiner and to understand Expressionism. In *Modern Architecture 1851-1945* (New York: Rizzoli, 1983), we watch Peter Frampton and Yukio Futagawa struggle mightily to get both right. Steiner appears briefly (but mistakenly) on pp. 156-157 in a chapter entitled "The Structure and Symbolism of Art Nouveau 1851-1914." Only after three derogatory and demonstrably false assertions in quick succession (the first Goetheanum was "the Anthroposophical cult building" and "the Anthroposophical church" and the place where "the Anthroposophical rite...based on Steiner's eurhythmic [*sic*] mystery plays" was to be performed) do the authors finally manage to admit that the site in Dornach came closer than any other to realizing the "Expressionist dream" and that the second Goetheanum is "one of the most striking sculptural concrete buildings of the twentieth century, anticipating to some degree Le Corbusier's Ronchamp Chapel to be built nearby, in the Jura, some thirty years later." We now know, of course, that the "anticipation" was no happy accident: as reported by witnesses, Le Corbusier's visit to Dornach in the late 1920s left him literally speechless. The other revealing phenomenon is Dennis Sharp's difficulty orienting himself relative to Steiner despite his important earlier study of 1966 (on which more below) in *Twentieth Century Architecture: A Visual History* (New York: Facts on File, 1991). Sharp mistakes the Goetheanum for a "temple," and quickly dismisses the revolutionary buildings surrounding it as "strange edifices connected with the movement," then throws up his hands, asserting that "Steiner's work falls into no stylistic category, its idiosyncrasies and originality makes [*sic*] it as unique as the Czech phase of Rondo-Cubism" (p. 51). And then of the second Goetheanum: "The expressionist work of Steiner defies normal critical evaluation. His personal style of 'soul architecture' transcends functional requirements or structural efficiencies. The Goetheanum II, replacing the earlier timber Goetheanum I, was the world's largest raw concrete building and was erected with the aid of sectional profile drawings. It remains one of the most amazing technical achievements of the twentieth century as well as one of its aesthetic curiosities" (p. 91).

A fascinating chapter in the reception of Steiner is the four-part series published by Mario Brunato and Sandro Mendini in *L'architettura*, vol. 6, Nos. 55-58 (1960), each with its own subtitle, but collected—rightly!—under the overarching title "Kultur espressionista." The first article, "Il primo Goetheanum a Dornach (1913)," is devoted to the first Goetheanum, and like all the installments, it is profusely illustrated with well-chosen photos of a very high quality (pp. 58-63). The next installment is devoted to the second Goetheanum (pp. 130-135), and the final two cover the many other buildings in the surrounding community (pp. 202-207 and 276-279). The texts are largely descriptive, and they make a sincere effort to understand Steiner's architecture on its own terms, often quoting his own words on the buildings.

There is an odd tension, however, between the respectful, largely accurate texts of the articles and the brief abstracts at the head of each installment, which are dismissive in tone and ill-informed: one wonders whether the abstracts were penned by someone other than the authors. For example, the English-language abstract of the initial essay refers to the "capriciously ondulated [*sic*] roof" of the first Goetheanum, and makes the wild (and mistaken) guess that "each form is determined by the symbols of good and evil" (p. 58). (Steiner insisted that there was no symbol to be found anywhere in the building.) And the English abstract of the final installment asserts that "Steiner, a great expressionist, designed a number of masterpieces, but opened no road for modern architecture" (p. 276). But the authors' final words say quite the opposite!: "Steiner is however a rare example of an architect-philosopher[*] who has brought to architecture a dramatic message of spirituality. In that sense, his architecture…can be useful and even profitable for anyone who is searching within architecture for intensity and veracity of expression" (p. 279). The second installment speaks of Steiner's "monumental and fully realized artistic conceptions"[†] (p. 131), and goes on to assert that his architecture "now shows itself to be profoundly relevant"[‡] (p. 134). Brunati and Mendini deserve tremendous credit for having penetrated so deeply into Steiner's challenging program, correctly identifying him as an Expressionist, and for having broken the seeming taboo against taking any Expressionist architect seriously (on which more below). Brunati and Mendini share with Kenneth Bayes the honor

---

[*] *un architetto-filosofo*
[†] *grandiose e raggiunte concezioni artistiche*
[‡] *ed esso si dimonstra ora di profonda attualità*

of having pioneered the scholarly study of Rudolf Steiner as an architect. Their influence on all subsequent studies is patent and important.

Another early but much briefer mention of Steiner can be found in Ulrich Conrads and Hans G. Sperlich, *The Architecture of Fantasy: Utopian Building and Planning in Modern Times* (New York: Praeger, 1962), which originally appeared in German in 1960. The authors juxtapose Steiner's first Goethea-num and Hans Poelzig's *Grosses Schauspielhaus* (1919) as both exemplifying "the architectural counterpart of the cave" and combining "grotto-like mys-teriousness with a rational program that is the result of studied intellectual endeavor" (p. 66). More insightful, but cryptic in its brevity, is their assertion that "Steiner sought a resonance of interior surfaces with the eurythmic feeling of the whole body in dance performance" (p. 66). Useful appendices con-tain a substantial and well-chosen excerpt from Steiner's slide lecture of June 29, 1921* (pp. 150-151) and a largely accurate biography of Steiner (which wrongly labels him a "cult leader" with "religious ideas," however).

Inspired both by Kenneth Bayes and the aforementioned series in *L'architet-tura*, Dennis Sharp devoted a chapter of his M.A. thesis (Liverpool University) to Rudolf Steiner, then published it as a freestanding essay,† "Rudolf Steiner and the way to a new style in architecture," *Architectural Association Journal*, June 1963, pp. 371-83. Sharp links him to Romantic modernism (the Am-sterdam school), the Berlin Expressionists, and van de Velde, while recognizing that "Steiner commanded a form language peculiarly his own" (p. 374). The concept of metamorphosis is put forward as central to that form language, and as "Steiner's unique contribution to modern architecture" (p. 374). He also sees parallels with Frank Lloyd Wright's notions of organic form.

Following on from the series by Brunati and Mendini, the Italian *Dizion-ario Enciclopedico di Architettura e Urbanistica*, ed. Paolo Portoghesi (Rome: Istituto Editoriale Romano, 1969), vol. 6, pp. 76-77, features an outstand-ing entry on Steiner. This refreshingly balanced and substantive early account identifies Steiner correctly as an Expressionist—indeed, the second Goethea-num is termed "an extreme example of an Expressionist edifice" and it rightly praises him as a "multifaceted personality" who possessed an "exceptional ar-tistic intuition," a strong technical background, and an acute sense of the problems of his age (pp. 76-77)

---

* CW 290; Conrads and Sperlich date it incorrectly as 25 June.
† See also the discussion of his book of 1966 below.

Eloquent Concrete: How Rudolf Steiner Employed Reinforced Concrete (London: Rudolf Steiner Press, 1979), 180 pp., by Rex Raab et al., described earlier in this essay, is a much more wide-ranging book than the title suggests. A very important component of this book is its account of the reception of Steiner's buildings by subsequent architects and historians of architecture, both in the initial chapter "Modern Architects Make a Discovery" and in the extensive bibliography at the end of the volume. (The reader should consult the latter as an important supplement to the present essay, as it lists many studies that cannot be discussed here, including notable work in Japanese by the architects Kenji Imai and Yuji Agematsu.)

Åke Fant and Arne Klingborg's *Der Unvollednete Functionalismus: Leben in der Architektur unserer Zeit* (Stuttgart: Verlag Urachhaus, 1985) devotes a prominent chapter to Rudolf Steiner, "Eine bemerkenswerte Bauunternehmung während des Ersten Weltkrieges," pp. 56-60. It is short, but appreciative; mostly it is descriptive. Another study of the same year, Michael Bockemühl's *Die Goetheaunumbauten in Dornach: Aspekte einer konkreten Architektur* (Stuttgart: Verlag Freies Geistesleben, 1985) was originally an inaugural lecture at the University of Bochum. This fine study also views Steiner's architecture through the lens of functionalism, but in a much-expanded sense of the term.

Caroline van Eck's otherwise admirable contribution *Organicism in nineteenth-century architecture: An inquiry into its theoretical and philosophical background* (Amsterdam: Architectura & Natura Press, 1994) cannot resist taking a gratuitous swipe at Steiner, even though he lies outside the study's chronological range. Perhaps she was grasping for excuses to establish delimiters that would keep a large topic manageable, which would explain why her opening chapter insists on a sharp distinction between nineteenth-century organicism and "its very distant relative, twentieth-century organic architecture, which was often inspired by pseudo-philosophies such as theosophy or Rudolf Steiner's anthroposophy" (p. 28). Needless to say, anyone who has actually studied Rudolf Steiner would take great exception to that characterization, and Steiner himself takes pains at every turn to stress the continuity between his work and Goethe's: that is, after all, the reason he named each of his two most important buildings "Goetheanum." Steiner comes off better towards the end of her study, where van Eck again distinguishes sharply between nineteenth- and twentieth-century organicism, but allows Steiner to appear in the august company of Frank Lloyd Wright and Alvar Aalto as exemplars of the latter. She asserts that the common denominator of twentieth-century organicism is opposition to architectural modernism, but there is no evidence of such opposition in Steiner's writings, and architectural Expressionism had its own agenda that developed simultaneously. In the lectures that have been collected in GA 288 (forthcoming as CW 288), Steiner shows appreciation for nineteenth-century organicism, and he mentions Gottfried Semper for example very positively. We know that as a young man enrolled at the *Technische Hochschule* in Vienna, Steiner was very impressed by Semper's student Ferstel. So it is that van Eck's study offers us invaluable help in understanding Steiner's predecessors who influenced his theories, but no help in understanding Steiner himself.

Kenneth Bayes's *Living Architecture: Rudolf Steiner's Ideas in Practice* (Edinburgh: Floris Books / Hudson, NY: Anthroposophic Press, 1994) is (unlike his earlier essay) quite an esoteric book, written by an anthroposophist and published by two different anthroposophical presses with an anthroposophical audience in mind. The context is large: Bayes situates Steiner relative to the great sweep of the history of architecture, including its future. While recognizing that many might take issue with them, I find the later chapters most compelling, in which Bayes argues that many of the iconic buildings of the later twentieth century (e.g. Saarinen's *TWA Terminal*, Scharoun's *Berlin Philharmonic*, and Utzon's *Sydney Opera House*) are part of an "organic stream" that includes Steiner as an important progenitor. In a different way, this later book is as pathbreaking as Bayes's essay of 1961.

Gary J. Coates's outstanding study *Eric Asmussen, architect* (Stockholm: Byggförlaget, 1997) contains a brief but excellent interlude on "Rudolf Steiner's Architectural Impulse" (pp. 160-165). Following David Adams, he sees Steiner as an "organic functionalist." "Central to Steiner's approach to design were his emphasis on the relationship between form and function and his belief that architecture for the present age should be based on the same formative principles that Goethe had discovered to be at work in the natural world ... Through buildings that were transparent expressions of their functions, the built environment would increasingly become more individualized, legible and meaningful" (p. 161). To Coates, Steiner's conception of function is broad: "For Steiner it involved an examination of a wide range of effects of the building on the human being, including the physical, emotional, aesthetic, psychological and spiritual" (p. 162). The Goetheanum incorporates four aspects of organic functionalism: "harmony with nature and the site, holism, metamorphosis, and the living wall" (p. 164).

Fiona Gray's article "Rudolf Steiner: Occult Crank or Architectural Mastermind?" *Architectural Theory Review*, 15:1 (2010), pp. 43-60, is beset by a systematic contradiction that reveals itself already in the abstract: she seems to want to accept uncritically the prevailing verdict that Steiner was an "eccentric oddity," and hence marginal, but she wants simultaneously to show that "the highly acclaimed works of many anthroposophically-inspired architects suggest that his gnostic perceptions may have something worthwhile to offer contemporary architecture" and that Steiner was "a source of inspiration for notable contemporary architects" (pp. 43; 44). These twin contentions are of course mutually exclusive. She uncritically echoes Colin Wilson's absurd complaint that Steiner's writings are "as unappetizing as dry toast" because he wrote like Goethe—tantamount to arguing that a composer's music is boring because it sounds so much like Beethoven! Steiner deserves better; mercifully he gets it as Gray's article progresses from gratuitous slights and speculations to solid architectural history (largely following Pehnt) and some excellent examples of contemporary architects who self-identify as anthroposophists, notably Imre Makovecz and Greg Burgess.

A beautiful volume is Rex Raab's *Offenbare Geheinisse: Vom Ursprung der Goetheanumbauten* (Dornach: Verlag am Goetheaum, 2011), 224 pp., which explores potential predecessors of the two Goetheanum buildings. The results are surprising: Raab finds echoes of Stonehenge, Solomon's Temple, Nordic stave churches, and the Artemision Temple in Ephesus, among others. The final two chapters are devoted to the two Goetheanums themselves, although Raab has little new to say about them.

Matthias Mochner, edited by Paul Schatz: *Architektur und Umstülpung: Studien zum organisch-dynamischen Raumbewußtsein* (Dornach: Verlag am Goetheanum, 2013), 431 pp., is a collection of many previously unpublished items by the mathematician Paul Schatz (1898-1979). Long, beautifully bound, with hundreds of colored plates, it is also very challenging and esoteric. It includes many previously unpublished essays from the early years of *Mensch und Baukunst* between 1954 and 1964, while it was still the privately circulated "Korrespondenz des Anthroposophischen Architektenkreises Stuttgart."

We have seen above that Expressionism has been actively ignored by architectural historians, or marginalized with derogatory labels such as "fantastic" or "ecstatic." Another way in which scholars have sought to marginalize the movement is by misrepresenting its ideals in ways lamented by the noted historian of Expressionist art, Rose-Carol Washton-Long:

> Where Expressionism was once equated with avant-garde modernism and experimentalism, with utopianism and internationalism, and with anarchism and socialism, it became characterized instead as apolitical, romantic, subjective, narcissistic, formless, and wildly irrational.*

It is high time that such distortions ended. Hence it is gratifying to discover that towards the end of the previous century scholars of the history of architecture finally began to give this "surgically removed" chapter the attention and respect that it deserves.

Following on the heels of Kenneth Bayes' seminal essay of 1961 we find an excellent short article by Ilse Meissner Reese on "Steiner's Goetheanum at Dornach," published in the journal *Progressive Architecture* in 1965 (vol. 46, Sept., p. 146). Reese clearly values Steiner as an architect, and she ascribes to him a "rare intuitive talent that many trained architects would envy." She echoes Bayes by drawing attention to Steiner in light of "the resurgence of interest in Art Nouveau and architectural expressionism." Although she initially deems Steiner "unclassifiable," Reese then argues that he is clearly related to Berg, Gaudì, Poelzig, and Mendelsohn, and she ultimately declares him to be "one of the purest examples of expressionist architecture."

Dennis Sharp included a slightly revised version of the aforementioned article of 1963 as a chapter with the same title in his important study *Modern Architecture and Expressionism* (New York: George Braziller, 1966), pp. 145-165. Many excellent photos are provided. Sharp's understanding of Steiner's architectural program is solid, which makes his mistaken characterization of anthroposophy as an "occult sect" and then a "pseudo-religious sect" (p. 147) all the more puzzling. Such derogatory labels (sadly common) are dou-

---

* Rose-Carol Washton-Long et al., *German Expressionism: Documents from the End of the Wilhelmine Empire to the Rise of National Socialism*, Documents of Twentieth-Century Art (Berkeley: U of California Press, 1993), p. xix.

bly unfortunate in that they are completely gratuitous, and they reveal only the authors' ignorance of Steiner's many other writings and lectures. Other odd assertions and wild speculations aside (e.g. that many of the forms were "powerfully erotic" and "perhaps unconscious fertility symbols" [p. 147], or that the roof of the first Goetheanum "bore an uncanny resemblance to German military headgear" [p. 152]—a real howler in light especially of Steiner's pacifist lectures in CW 287 and elsewhere), Sharp is quite astute about the fundamentals of Steiner's architectural theory, focusing on the Expressionist context and Steiner's profound debts to Goethe's scientific work.

Jacques Gubler's "Beton et architecture: trois propositions des années 1925," *Werk*, 58 (May 1971), pp. 350-353, compares Steiner's second Goetheaum with buildings by Hans Schmidt and Peter Meyer. It doesn't do more than describe the building, but it does so accurately. An English-language summary was published with the title "Concrete Interlude" in *Architectural Design*, 41 (July 1971), pp. 429-430.

Like Sharp's book of 1966, Wolfgang Pehnt's now-classic study *Expressionist Architecture* (New York: Praeger, 1973; German edn. Stuttgart: Verlag Gerd Hatje, 1973) devotes an entire chapter to Rudolf Steiner (pp. 137-148). Pehnt's chapter is admirably succinct and accurate, and he rightly emphasizes the spiritual underpinnings of Steiner's theories. Steiner's close relationship to other contemporary architects, whom we now view retrospectively as "Expressionist," is well documented, yet for all that Steiner remains *sui generis*, Pehnt argues. Steiner's protestations that his architecture is not "symbolic" are met with justified skepticism, and Pehnt is understandably put off by a lack of independent thinking among many of Steiner's followers. Yet Pehnt also goes out of his way to correct what he sees as a devaluation of the second Goetheanum by anthroposophists, calling it "one of the most magnificent pieces of sculptural architecture of the twentieth century" (p. 148). Indeed, Pehnt's later volume on Steiner as an architect focuses on the second Goetheanum, and it is among the very best treatments available. One dimension that is still lacking here (made good by Raab et al. in *Eloquent Concrete*, discussed above) is the degree to which Steiner influenced important later architects such as Le Corbusier and Frank Lloyd Wright,[†] but on the whole this is a full and fair treatment of Steiner's work that situates him properly

---

† See also John Kettle's Introduction to the present volume.

within both Expressionism and the overarching history of twentieth century architecture. Further discussion of Steiner along the same lines can be found in Wolfgang Pehnt, "Anthroposophische Architektur," in *Die Architektur des Expressionismus* (Ostfildern: Hatje Cantz, 1998).

Harald Seemann's *Der Hang zum Gesamtkunstwerk: Europäischen Utopien set 1800* (Aarau and Frankfurt am Main: Verlag Sauerländer, 1983) contains a section on Steiner on pp. 221-230. After a short introduction, this section consists entirely of quotes from Steiner that provide an excellent basis for understanding his aesthetic sense.

In the otherwise outstanding catalogue *Expressionist Utopias: Paradise: Metropolis: Architectural Fantasy*, ed. Timothy O. Benson (Berkeley: U of California P, 1994), Rudolf Steiner garners only one passing reference, while even the single plate devoted to the first Goetheanum is not discussed at all. Ralf Beil and Claudia Dillmann likewise miss a great opportunity to discuss Rudolf Steiner's architecture (not to mention eurythmy and his other artistic work!) in the ambitious volume they edited, *The Total Artwork in Expressionism: Art, Film, Literature, Theater, Dance, and Architecture, 1905-1925* (Ostfildern: Hatje Cantz, 2011). The catalogue was issued with an accompanying DVD, *The Total Artwork in Expressionism: Art to Hear Series.* Aside from two references in passing to Steiner's influence on Arnold Schönberg and Johannes Itten (pp. 319 and 408 respectively), and a single plate with a detail of the second Goetheanum (p. 378), there is only a single substantive reference to Steiner, on p. 379. There we learn only that the second Goetheanum was "one of the most curious architectural sculptures of the time," that Steiner had gotten to know "mystical" and "fantastical" members of the circle around Otto Wagner while in Vienna, that he loved the "odd novels" of the science fiction writer Paul Scheerbart, and that he "enjoyed staying overnight with friends on the Old Town Square in Prague where, before his eyes, he had a magnum opus of this sharp-edged, crystalline style ['the cubistic architecture of the young Czechs'], with the House at the Black Madonna department store." It is disappointing indeed that Steiner was not discussed more extensively in this splendid volume, issued so long after the definitive architectural histories by Sharp and Pehnt discussed immediately above, and also in light of the special issue of the Zürich journal *Werk* (August, 1960), devoted to "The Synthesis of the Arts" that included an article by Willy Rotzler, "Das Goetheanum in Dornach als Beispiel der Integration der Künste" ["The Goetheanum in Dornach as an Example of the Integration of the Arts"]. As was noted above, despite their other wild misconceptions about Steiner, even Peter Frampton and Yukio Futagawa saw clearly that Steiner came closer than anyone else to realizing the Expressionist dream of a *Gesamtkunstwerk* in Dornach.

Ákos Moravánsky's article "Il libero muoversi dello spirito fra le curve in cemento del Goetheanum di Rudolf Steiner / Free Movement of the Spirit among the Concrete Curves of Rudolf Steiner's Goetheanum," *Domus*, 944 (Feb. 2011) pp. 70-78, in both Italian and English, has beautiful plans and color plates. He carefully describes how Steiner differs from Antonio Gaudi, Gottfried Semper, and his student Joseph Bayer.

We have seen above how crucial it was when Kenneth Bayes recognized that there cannot be a single "master narrative" (neither anointed school nor teleology, as Jencks put it) in the history of twentieth-century architecture, but rather one must trace at least two streams: the International Style and Expressionism.* My own contention is that Rudolf Steiner's architecture is a prime exemplar—arguably *the* prime exemplar—of at least eight central tenets of architectural Expressionism: transcendence through transformation, rejection of historical forms, organicism, representation of inner states and unconscious forces, direct appeals to feeling and will, utopianism, transparency, and a striving to attain the *Gesamtkunstwerk* or union of all the arts. Hence the intention of the English translations of CW 287, CW 288, and CW 290 is not just to raise awareness of Steiner himself, but to contribute to a greater appreciation and understanding of the larger "Expressionist" movement of which he is a part.

If Kenneth Bayes, Rex Raab, Fiona Gray, and others are right that many of the most iconic buildings of the late twentieth century could very well be described as "Expressionist" in a broad sense, and if Rudolf Steiner was arguably the greatest of the early Expressionist architects (as Scharoun himself asserted), then might it not be said that Rudolf Steiner has been unjustly neglected by mainstream scholarship? And more: Was he not a great architectural pioneer?

---

* Kenneth Bayes, "Architecture in Accord with Man," in A.C. Harwood, ed., The Faithful Thinker (London: Hodder and Stoughton, 1961), pp. 163-178.

RUDOLF STEINER'S COLLECTED WORKS

The German Edition of Rudolf Steiner's Collected Works (the *Gesamtausgabe* [GA] published by Rudolf Steiner Verlag, Dornach, Switzerland) presently runs to 354 titles, organized either by type of work (written or spoken), chronology, audience (public or other), or subject (education, art, etc.). For ease of comparison, the Collected Works in English [CW] follows the German organization. A complete listing of the CWs follows with *literal translations* of the German titles. Other than in the case of the books published in his lifetime, titles were rarely given by Rudolf Steiner himself, and were often provided by the editors of the German editions. The titles in English are not necessarily the same as the German; and, indeed, over the past seventy-five years have frequently been different, with the same book sometimes appearing under different titles.

For ease of identification and to avoid confusion, we suggest that readers looking for a title should do so by CW number. Because the work of creating the Collected Works of Rudolf Steiner is an ongoing process, with new titles being published every year, we have not indicated in this listing which books are presently available. To find out what titles in the Collected Works are currently in print, please check our website at www.steinerbooks.org, or write to: SteinerBooks; 610 Main Street, Great Barrington, MA 01230.

A. Written Work

I. Writings 1884–1925

CW 1   Goethe: Natural-Scientific Writings, Introduction, with Footnotes and Explanations in the text by Rudolf Steiner

CW 2   Outlines of an Epistemology of the Goethean World View, with Special Consideration of Schiller

CW 3   Truth and Science

CW 4   The Philosophy of Freedom

CW 4a   Documents to "The Philosophy of Freedom"

CW 5   Friedrich Nietzsche, A Fighter against His Own Time

CW 6   Goethe's Worldview

CW 6a   *[Now in CW 30]*

CW 7   Mysticism at the Dawn of Modern Spiritual Life and Its Relationship with Modern Worldviews

CW 8   Christianity as Mystical Fact and the Mysteries of Antiquity

CW 9   Theosophy: An Introduction into Supersensible World Knowledge and Human Purpose

CW 10   How Does One Attain Knowledge of Higher Worlds?

CW 11   From the Akasha-Chronicle

CW 12   Levels of Higher Knowledge

CW 13   Occult Science in Outline

CW 14   Four Mystery Dramas

CW 15   The Spiritual Guidance of the Individual and Humanity

CW 16   A Way to Human Self-Knowledge: Eight Meditations

CW 17   The Threshold of the Spiritual World. Aphoristic Comments

CW 18   The Riddles of Philosophy in Their History, Presented as an Outline

CW 54	The Riddles of the World and Anthroposophy
CW 55	Knowledge of the Supersensible in Our Times and Its Meaning for Life Today
CW 56	Knowledge of the Soul and of the Spirit
CW 57	Where and How Does One Find the Spirit?
CW 58	The Metamorphoses of the Soul Life. Paths of Soul Experiences: Part One
CW 59	The Metamorphoses of the Soul Life. Paths of Soul Experiences: Part Two
CW 60	The Answers of Spiritual Science to the Biggest Questions of Existence
CW 61	Human History in the Light of Spiritual Research
CW 62	Results of Spiritual Research
CW 63	Spiritual Science as a Treasure for Life
CW 64	Out of Destiny-Burdened Times
CW 65	Out of Central European Spiritual Life
CW 66	Spirit and Matter, Life and Death
CW 67	The Eternal in the Human Soul. Immortality and Freedom
CW 68	Public lectures in various cities, 1906-1918
CW 69	Public lectures in various cities, 1906-1918
CW 70	Public lectures in various cities, 1906-1918
CW 71	Public lectures in various cities, 1906-1918
CW 72	Freedom – Immortality – Social Life
CW 73	The Supplementing of the Modern Sciences through Anthroposophy
CW 73a	Specialized Fields of Knowledge and Anthroposophy
CW 74	The Philosophy of Thomas Aquinas
CW 75	Public lectures in various cities, 1906-1918
CW 76	The Fructifying Effect of Anthroposophy on Specialized Fields
CW 77a	The Task of Anthroposophy in Relation to Science and Life: The Darmstadt College Course
CW 77b	Art and Anthroposophy. The Goetheanum-Impulse
CW 78	Anthroposophy, Its Roots of Knowledge and Fruits for Life
CW 79	The Reality of the Higher Worlds
CW 80	Public lectures in various cities, 1922
CW 81	Renewal-Impulses for Culture and Science–Berlin College Course
CW 82	So that the Human Being Can Become a Complete Human Being
CW 83	Western and Eastern World-Contrast. Paths to Understanding It through Anthroposophy
CW 84	What Did the Goetheanum Intend and What Should Anthroposophy Do?

II. Lectures to the Members of the Anthroposophical Society

CW 88	Concerning the Astral World and Devachan
CW 89	Consciousness – Life – Form. Fundamental Principles of a Spiritual-Scientific Cosmology
CW 90	Participant Notes from the Lectures during the Years 1903-1905
CW 91	Participant Notes from the Lectures during the Years 1903-1905
CW 92	The Occult Truths of Ancient Myths and Sagas
CW 93	The Temple Legend and the Golden Legend
CW 93a	Fundamentals of Esotericism

CW 264	On the History and the Contents of the First Section of the Esoteric School from 1904 to 1914. Letters, Newsletters, Documents, Lectures
CW 265	On the History and from the Contents of the Ritual-Knowledge Section of the Esoteric School from 1904 to 1914. Documents, and Lectures from the Years 1906 to 1914, as Well as on New Approaches to Ritual-Knowledge Work in the Years 1921-1924
CW 266/1	From the Contents of the Esoteric Lessons. Volume 1: 1904-1909. Notes from Memory of Participants. Meditation texts from the notes of Rudolf Steiner
CW 266/2	From the Contents of the Esoteric Lessons. Volume 2: 1910-1912. Notes from Memory of Participants
CW 266/3	From the Contents of the Esoteric Lessons. Volume 3: 1913, 1914 and 1920-1923. Notes from Memory of Participants. Meditation texts from the notes of Rudolf Steiner
CW 267	Soul-Exercises: Vol. 1: Exercises with Word and Image Meditations for the Methodological Development of Higher Powers of Knowledge, 1904-1924
CW 268	Soul-Exercises: Vol. 2: Mantric Verses, 1903-1925
CW 269	Ritual Texts for the Celebration of the Free Christian Religious Instruction. The Collected Verses for Teachers and Students of the Waldorf School
CW 270	Esoteric Instructions for the First Class of the School for Spiritual Science at the Goetheanum 1924, 4 Volumes

III. Lectures and Courses on Specific Realms of Life

Lectures on Art

CW 271	Art and Knowledge of Art. Foundations of a New Aesthetic
CW 272	Spiritual-Scientific Commentary on Goethe's "Faust" in Two Volumes. Vol. 1: Faust, the Striving Human Being
CW 273	Spiritual-Scientific Commentary on Goethe's "Faust" in Two Volumes. Vol. 2: The Faust-Problem
CW 274	Addresses for the Christmas Plays from the Old Folk Traditions
CW 275	Art in the Light of Mystery Wisdom
CW 276	The Artistic in Its Mission in the World. The Genius of Language. The World of Self-Revealing Radiant Appearances – Anthroposophy and Art. Anthroposophy and Poetry
CW 277	Eurythmy. The Revelation of the Speaking Soul
CW 277a	The Origin and Development of Eurythmy
CW 278	Eurythmy as Visible Song
CW 279	Eurythmy as Visible Speech
CW 280	The Method and Nature of Speech Formation
CW 281	The Art of Recitation and Declamation
CW 282	Speech Formation and Dramatic Art
CW 283	The Nature of Things Musical and the Experience of Tone in the Human Being
CW 284/285	Images of Occult Seals and Pillars. The Munich Congress of Whitsun 1907 and Its Consequences
CW 286	Paths to a New Style of Architecture. "And the Building Becomes Human"
CW 287	The Building at Dornach as a Symbol of Historical Becoming and an Artistic Transformation Impulse

CW 288	Style-Forms in the Living Organic
CW 289	The Building-Idea of the Goetheanum: Lectures with Slides from the Years 1920-1921
CW 290	The Building-Idea of the Goetheanum: Lectures with Slides from the Years 1920-1921
CW 291	The Nature of Colors
CW 291a	Knowledge of Colors. Supplementary Volume to "The Nature of Colors"
CW 292	Art History as Image of Inner Spiritual Impulses

Lectures on Education

CW 293	General Knowledge of the Human Being as the Foundation of Pedagogy
CW 294	The Art of Education, Methodology and Didactics
CW 295	The Art of Education: Seminar Discussions and Lectures on Lesson Planning
CW 296	The Question of Education as a Social Question
CW 297	The Idea and Practice of the Waldorf School
CW 297a	Education for Life: Self-Education and the Practice of Pedagogy
CW 298	Rudolf Steiner in the Waldorf School
CW 299	Spiritual-Scientific Observations on Speech
CW 300a	Conferences with the Teachers of the Free Waldorf School in Stuttgart, 1919 to 1924, in 3 Volumes, Vol. 1
CW 300b	Conferences with the Teachers of the Free Waldorf School in Stuttgart, 1919 to 1924, in 3 Volumes, Vol. 2
CW 300c	Conferences with the Teachers of the Free Waldorf School in Stuttgart, 1919 to 1924, in 3 Volumes, Vol. 3
CW 301	The Renewal of Pedagogical-Didactical Art through Spiritual Science
CW 302	Knowledge of the Human Being and the Forming of Class Lessons
CW 302a	Education and Teaching from a Knowledge of the Human Being
CW 303	The Healthy Development of the Human Being
CW 304	Methods of Education and Teaching Based on Anthroposophy
CW 304a	Anthroposophical Knowledge of the Human Being and Pedagogy
CW 305	The Soul-Spiritual Foundational Forces of the Art of Education. Spiritual Values in Education and Social Life
CW 306	Pedagogical Praxis from the Viewpoint of a Spiritual-Scientific Knowledge of the Human Being. The Education of the Child and Young Human Beings
CW 307	The Spiritual Life of the Present and Education
CW 308	The Method of Teaching and the Life-Requirements for Teaching
CW 309	Anthroposophical Pedagogy and Its Prerequisites
CW 310	The Pedagogical Value of a Knowledge of the Human Being and the Cultural Value of Pedagogy
CW 311	The Art of Education from an Understanding of the Being of Humanity

Lectures on Medicine

CW 312	Spiritual Science and Medicine
CW 313	Spiritual-Scientific Viewpoints on Therapy
CW 314	Physiology and Therapy Based on Spiritual Science
CW 315	Curative Eurythmy

CW 340	The National-Economics Course. The Tasks of a New Science of Economics, Volume 1
CW 341	The National-Economics Seminar. The Tasks of a New Science of Economics, Volume 2

Lectures and Courses on Christian Religious Work

CW 342	Lectures and Courses on Christian Religious Work, Vol. 1: Anthroposophical Foundations for a Renewed Christian Religious Working
CW 343	Lectures and Courses on Christian Religious Work, Vol. 2: Spiritual Knowledge – Religious Feeling – Cultic Doing
CW 344	Lectures and Courses on Christian Religious Work, Vol. 3: Lectures at the Founding of the Christian Community
CW 345	Lectures and Courses on Christian Religious Work, Vol. 4: Concerning the Nature of the Working Word
CW 346	Lectures and Courses on Christian Religious Work, Vol. 5: The Apocalypse and the Work of the Priest

Lectures for Workers at the Goetheanum

CW 347	The Knowledge of the Nature of the Human Being According to Body, Soul and Spirit. On Earlier Conditions of the Earth
CW 348	On Health and Illness. Foundations of a Spiritual-Scientific Doctrine of the Senses
CW 349	On the Life of the Human Being and of the Earth. On the Nature of Christianity
CW 350	Rhythms in the Cosmos and in the Human Being. How Does One Come To See the Spiritual World?
CW 351	The Human Being and the World. The Influence of the Spirit in Nature. On the Nature of Bees
CW 352	Nature and the Human Being Observed Spiritual-Scientifically
CW 353	The History of Humanity and the World-Views of the Folk Cultures
CW 354	The Creation of the World and the Human Being. Life on Earth and the Influence of the Stars

SIGNIFICANT EVENTS
IN THE LIFE OF RUDOLF STEINER

1829:   June 23: birth of Johann Steiner (1829-1910)—Rudolf Steiner's father—in Geras, Lower Austria.

1834:   May 8: birth of Franciska Blie (1834-1918)—Rudolf Steiner's mother—in Horn, Lower Austria. "My father and mother were both children of the glorious Lower Austrian forest district north of the Danube."

1860:   May 16: marriage of Johann Steiner and Franciska Blie.

1861:   February 25: birth of *Rudolf Joseph Lorenz Steiner* in Kraljevec, Croatia, near the border with Hungary, where Johann Steiner works as a telegrapher for the South Austria Railroad. Rudolf Steiner is baptized two days later, February 27, the date usually given as his birthday.

1862:   Summer: the family moves to Mödling, Lower Austria.

1863:   The family moves to Pottschach, Lower Austria, near the Styrian border, where Johann Steiner becomes stationmaster. "The view stretched to the mountains... majestic peaks in the distance and the sweet charm of nature in the immediate surroundings."

1864:   November 15: birth of Rudolf Steiner's sister, Leopoldine (d. November 1, 1927). She will become a seamstress and live with her parents for the rest of her life.

1866:   July 28: birth of Rudolf Steiner's deaf-mute brother, Gustav (d. May 1, 1941).

1867:   Rudolf Steiner enters the village school. Following a disagreement between his father and the schoolmaster, whose wife falsely accused the boy of causing a commotion, Rudolf Steiner is taken out of school and taught at home.

1868:   A critical experience. Unknown to the family, an aunt dies in a distant town. Sitting in the station waiting room, Rudolf Steiner sees her "form," which speaks to him, asking for help. "Beginning with this experience, a new soul life began in the boy, one in which not only the outer trees and mountains spoke to him, but also the worlds that lay behind them. From this moment on, the boy began to live with the spirits of nature...."

1869:   The family moves to the peaceful, rural village of Neudorfl, near Wiener-Neustadt in present-day Austria. Rudolf Steiner attends the village school. Because of the "unorthodoxy" of his writing and spelling, he has to do "extra lessons."

1870:   Through a book lent to him by his tutor, he discovers geometry: "To grasp something purely in the spirit brought me inner happiness. I know that I first learned happiness through geometry." The same tutor allows him to draw, while other students still struggle with their reading and writing. "An artistic element" thus enters his education.

1871:   Though his parents are not religious, Rudolf Steiner becomes a "church child," a favorite of the priest, who was "an exceptional character." "Up to the age of ten or eleven, among those I came to know, he was far and away the most significant." Among other things, he introduces Steiner to Copernican, heliocentric cosmology. As an altar boy, Rudolf Steiner serves at Masses, funerals, and Corpus Christi processions. At year's end, after an incident in which he escapes a thrashing, his father forbids him to go to church.

1872:   Rudolf Steiner transfers to grammar school in Wiener-Neustadt, a five-mile walk from home, which must be done in all weathers.

1873-75: Through his teachers and on his own, Rudolf Steiner has many wonderful experiences with science and mathematics. Outside school, he teaches himself analytic geometry, trigonometry, differential equations, and calculus.

1876:   Rudolf Steiner begins tutoring other students. He learns bookbinding from his father. He also teaches himself stenography.

1877:   Rudolf Steiner discovers Kant's *Critique of Pure Reason*, which he reads and rereads. He also discovers and reads von Rotteck's *World History*.

1878:   He studies extensively in contemporary psychology and philosophy.

1879:   Rudolf Steiner graduates from high school with honors. His father is transferred to Inzersdorf, near Vienna. He uses his first visit to Vienna "to purchase a great number of philosophy books"—Kant, Fichte, Schelling, and Hegel, as well as numerous histories of philosophy. His aim: to find a path from the "I" to nature.

October 1879-1883: Rudolf Steiner attends the Technical College in Vienna—to study mathematics, chemistry, physics, mineralogy, botany, zoology, biology, geology, and mechanics—with a scholarship. He also attends lectures in history and literature, while avidly reading philosophy on his own. His two favorite professors are Karl Julius Schröer (German language and literature) and Edmund Reitlinger (physics). He also audits lectures by Robert Zimmerman on aesthetics and Franz Brentano on philosophy. During this year he begins his friendship with Moritz Zitter (1861-1921), who will help support him financially when he is in Berlin.

1880:   Rudolf Steiner attends lectures on Schiller and Goethe by Karl Julius Schröer, who becomes his mentor. Also "through a remarkable combination of circumstances," he meets Felix Koguzki, a "herb gatherer" and healer, who could "see deeply into the secrets of nature." Rudolf Steiner will meet and study with this "emissary of the Master" throughout his time in Vienna.

1881:   January: "… I didn't sleep a wink. I was busy with philosophical problems until about 12:30 a.m. Then, finally, I threw myself down on my couch. All my striving during the previous year had been to research whether the following statement by Schelling was true or not: *Within everyone dwells a secret, marvelous capacity to draw back from the stream of time—out of the self clothed in all that comes to us from outside—into our innermost being and there, in the immutable form of the Eternal, to look into ourselves.* I believe, and I am still quite certain of it, that I discovered this capacity in myself; I had long had an inkling of it. Now the whole of idealist philosophy stood before me in modified form. What's a sleepless night compared to that!"

          Rudolf Steiner begins communicating with leading thinkers of the day, who send him books in return, which he reads eagerly.

July: "I am not one of those who dives into the day like an animal in human form. I pursue a quite specific goal, an idealistic aim—knowledge of the truth! This cannot be done offhandedly. It requires the greatest striving in the world, free of all egotism, and equally of all resignation."

August: Steiner puts down on paper for the first time thoughts for a "Philosophy of Freedom." "The striving for the absolute: this human yearning is freedom." He also seeks to outline a "peasant philosophy," describing what the worldview of a "peasant"—one who lives close to the earth and the old ways—really is.

1881-1882: Felix Koguzki, the herb gatherer, reveals himself to be the envoy of another, higher initiatory personality, who instructs Rudolf Steiner to penetrate Fichte's philosophy and to master modern scientific thinking as a preparation for right entry into the spirit. This "Master" also teaches him the double (evolutionary and involutionary) nature of time.

1882: Through the offices of Karl Julius Schröer, Rudolf Steiner is asked by Joseph Kurschner to edit Goethe's scientific works for the *Deutschen National-Literatur* edition. He writes "A Possible Critique of Atomistic Concepts" and sends it to Friedrich Theodore Vischer.

1883: Rudolf Steiner completes his college studies and begins work on the Goethe project.

1884: First volume of Goethe's *Scientific Writings* (CW 1) appears (March). He lectures on Goethe and Lessing, and Goethe's approach to science. In July, he enters the household of Ladislaus and Pauline Specht as tutor to the four Specht boys. He will live there until 1890. At this time, he meets Josef Breuer (1842-1925), the coauthor with Sigmund Freud of *Studies in Hysteria*, who is the Specht family doctor.

1885: While continuing to edit Goethe's writings, Rudolf Steiner reads deeply in contemporary philosophy (Edouard von Hartmann, Johannes Volkelt, and Richard Wahle, among others).

1886: May: Rudolf Steiner sends Kurschner the manuscript of *Outlines of Goethe's Theory of Knowledge* (CW 2), which appears in October, and which he sends out widely. He also meets the poet Marie Eugenie Delle Grazie and writes "Nature and Our Ideals" for her. He attends her salon, where he meets many priests, theologians, and philosophers, who will become his friends. Meanwhile, the director of the Goethe Archive in Weimar requests his collaboration with the *Sophien* edition of Goethe's works, particularly the writings on color.

1887: At the beginning of the year, Rudolf Steiner is very sick. As the year progresses and his health improves, he becomes increasingly "a man of letters," lecturing, writing essays, and taking part in Austrian cultural life. In August-September, the second volume of Goethe's *Scientific Writings* appears.

1888: January-July: Rudolf Steiner assumes editorship of the "German Weekly" (*Deutsche Wochenschrift*). He begins lecturing more intensively, giving, for example, a lecture titled "Goethe as Father of a New Aesthetics." He meets and becomes soul friends with Friedrich Eckstein (1861-1939), a vegetarian, philosopher of symbolism, alchemist, and musician, who will introduce him to various spiritual currents (including Theosophy) and with whom he will meditate and interpret esoteric and alchemical texts.

1889: Rudolf Steiner first reads Nietzsche (*Beyond Good and Evil*). He encounters Theosophy again and learns of Madame Blavatsky in the Theosophical circle around Marie Lang (1858-1934). Here he also meets well-known figures of Austrian life, as well as esoteric figures like the occultist Franz Hartman and Karl Leinigen-Billigen (translator of C.G. Harrison's *The Transcendental Universe*.) During this period, Steiner first reads A.P. Sinnett's *Esoteric Buddhism* and Mabel Collins's *Light on the Path*. He also begins traveling, visiting Budapest, Weimar, and Berlin (where he meets philosopher Edouard von Hartmann).

1890: Rudolf Steiner finishes volume 3 of Goethe's scientific writings. He begins his doctoral dissertation, which will become *Truth and Science* (CW 3). He also meets the poet and feminist Rosa Mayreder (1858-1938), with whom he can exchange his most intimate thoughts. In September, Rudolf Steiner moves to Weimar to work in the Goethe-Schiller Archive.

1891: Volume 3 of the Kurschner edition of Goethe appears. Meanwhile, Rudolf Steiner edits Goethe's studies in mineralogy and scientific writings for the *Sophien* edition. He meets Ludwig Laistner of the Cotta Publishing Company, who asks for a book on the basic question of metaphysics. From this will result, ultimately, *The Philosophy of Freedom* (CW 4), which will be published not by Cotta but by Emil Felber. In October, Rudolf Steiner takes the oral exam for a doctorate in philosophy, mathematics, and mechanics at Rostock University, receiving his doctorate on the twenty-sixth. In November, he gives his first lecture on Goethe's "Fairy Tale" in Vienna.

1892: Rudolf Steiner continues work at the Goethe-Schiller Archive and on his *Philosophy of Freedom. Truth and Science*, his doctoral dissertation, is published. Steiner undertakes to write introductions to books on Schopenhauer and Jean Paul for Cotta. At year's end, he finds lodging with Anna Eunike, née Schulz (1853-1911), a widow with four daughters and a son. He also develops a friendship with Otto Erich Hartleben (1864-1905) with whom he shares literary interests.

1893: Rudolf Steiner begins his habit of producing many reviews and articles. In March, he gives a lecture titled "Hypnotism, with Reference to Spiritism." In September, volume 4 of the Kurschner edition is completed. In November, *The Philosophy of Freedom* appears. This year, too, he meets John Henry Mackay (1864-1933), the anarchist, scholar, and biographer of Max Stirner.

1894: Rudolf Steiner meets Elisabeth Förster Nietzsche, the philosopher's sister, and begins to read Nietzsche in earnest, beginning with the as yet unpublished *Antichrist*. He also meets Ernst Haeckel (1834-1919). In the fall, he begins to write *Nietzsche, A Fighter against His Time* (CW 5).

1895: May, *Nietzsche, A Fighter against His Time* appears.

1896: January 22: Rudolf Steiner sees Friedrich Nietzsche for the first and only time. Moves between the Nietzsche and the Goethe-Schiller Archives, where he completes his work before year's end. He falls out with Elisabeth Förster Nietzsche, thus ending his association with the Nietzsche Archive.

1897: Rudolf Steiner finishes the manuscript of *Goethe's Worldview* (CW 6). He moves to Berlin with Anna Eunike and begins editorship of the *Magazin fur Literatur*. From now on, Steiner will write countless reviews, literary and philosophical articles, and so on. He begins lecturing at the "Free Literary Society." In September, he attends the Zionist Congress in Basel. He sides with Dreyfus in the Dreyfus affair.

1898: Rudolf Steiner is very active as an editor in the political, artistic, and theatrical life of Berlin. He becomes friendly with John Henry Mackay and poet Ludwig Jacobowski (1868-1900). He joins Jacobowski's circle of writers, artists, and scientists—"The Coming Ones" (*Die Kommenden*)—and contributes lectures to the group until 1903. He also lectures at the "League for College Pedagogy." He writes an article for Goethe's sesquicentennial, "Goethe's Secret Revelation," on the "Fairy Tale of the Green Snake and the Beautiful Lily."

1898-99: "This was a trying time for my soul as I looked at Christianity.... I was able to progress only by contemplating, by means of spiritual perception, the evolution of Christianity .... Conscious knowledge of real Christianity began to dawn in me around the turn of the century. This seed continued to develop. My soul trial occurred shortly before the beginning of the twentieth century. It was decisive for my soul's development that I stood spiritually before the Mystery of Golgotha in a deep and solemn celebration of knowledge."

1899: Rudolf Steiner begins teaching and giving lectures and lecture cycles at the Workers' College, founded by Wilhelm Liebknecht (1826-1900). He will continue to do so until 1904. Writes: *Literature and Spiritual Life in the Nineteenth Century; Individualism in Philosophy; Haeckel and His Opponents; Poetry in the Present;* and begins what will become (fifteen years later) *The Riddles of Philosophy* (CW 18). He also meets many artists and writers, including Käthe Kollwitz, Stefan Zweig, and Rainer Maria Rilke. On October 31, he marries Anna Eunike.

1900: "I thought that the turn of the century must bring humanity a new light. It seemed to me that the separation of human thinking and willing from the spirit had peaked. A turn or reversal of direction in human evolution seemed to me a necessity." Rudolf Steiner finishes *World and Life Views in the Nineteenth Century* (the second part of what will become *The Riddles of Philosophy*) and dedicates it to Ernst Haeckel. It is published in March. He continues lecturing at *Die Kommenden*, whose leadership he assumes after the death of Jacobowski. Also, he gives the Gutenberg Jubilee lecture before 7,000 typesetters and printers. In September, Rudolf Steiner is invited by Count and Countess Brockdorff to lecture in the Theosophical Library. His first lecture is on Nietzsche. His second lecture is titled "Goethe's Secret Revelation." October 6, he begins a lecture cycle on the mystics that will become *Mystics after Modernism* (CW 7). November-December: "Marie von Sivers appears in the audience...." Also in November, Steiner gives his first lecture at the Giordano Bruno Bund (where he will continue to lecture until May, 1905). He speaks on Bruno and modern Rome, focusing on the importance of the philosophy of Thomas Aquinas as monism.

1901: In continual financial straits, Rudolf Steiner's early friends Moritz Zitter and Rosa Mayreder help support him. In October, he begins the lecture cycle *Christianity as Mystical Fact* (CW 8) at the Theosophical Library. In November, he gives his first "Theosophical lecture" on Goethe's "Fairy Tale" in Hamburg at the invitation of Wilhelm Hubbe-Schleiden. He also attends a gathering to celebrate the founding of the Theosophical Society at Count and Countess Brockdorff's. He gives a lecture cycle, "From Buddha to Christ," for the circle of the *Kommenden*. November 17, Marie von Sivers asks Rudolf Steiner if Theosophy needs a Western-Christian spiritual movement (to complement Theosophy's Eastern emphasis). "The question was posed. Now, following spiritual laws, I could begin to give an answer...." In December, Rudolf Steiner writes his first article for a Theosophical publication. At year's end, the Brockdorffs and possibly Wilhelm Hubbe-Schleiden ask Rudolf Steiner to join the Theosophical Society and undertake the leadership of the German section. Rudolf Steiner agrees, on the condition that Marie von Sivers (then in Italy) work with him.

1902: Beginning in January, Rudolf Steiner attends the opening of the Workers' School in Spandau with Rosa Luxemberg (1870-1919). January 17, Rudolf Steiner joins the Theosophical Society. In April, he is asked to become general secretary of the German Section of the Theosophical Society, and works on preparations for its founding. In July, he visits London for a Theosophical congress. He meets Bertram Keightly, G.R.S. Mead, A.P. Sinnett, and Annie Besant, among others. In September, *Christianity as Mystical Fact* appears. In October, Rudolf Steiner gives his first public lecture on Theosophy ("Monism and Theosophy") to about three hundred people at the Giordano Bruno Bund. On October 19-21, the German Section of the Theosophical Society has its first meeting; Rudolf Steiner is the general secretary, and Annie Besant attends. Steiner lectures on practical karma studies. On October 23, Annie Besant inducts Rudolf Steiner into the Esoteric School of the Theosophical Society. On October 25, Steiner begins a weekly series of lectures: "The Field of Theosophy." During this year, Rudolf Steiner also meets Ita Wegman (1876-1943), who will become his close collaborator in his final years.

1903: Rudolf Steiner holds about 300 lectures and seminars. In May, the first issue of the periodical *Luzifer* appears. In June, Rudolf Steiner visits London for the first meeting of the Federation of the European Sections of the Theosophical Society, where he meets Colonel Olcott. He begins to write *Theosophy* (CW 9).

1904: Rudolf Steiner continues lecturing at the Workers' College and elsewhere (about 90 lectures), while lecturing intensively all over Germany among Theosophists (about 140 lectures). In February, he meets Carl Unger (1878-1929), who will become a member of the board of the Anthroposophical Society (1913). In March, he meets Michael Bauer (1871-1929), a Christian mystic, who will also be on the board. In May, *Theosophy* appears, with the dedication: "To the spirit of Giordano Bruno." Rudolf Steiner and Marie von Sivers visit London for meetings with Annie Besant. June: Rudolf Steiner and Marie von Sivers attend the meeting of the Federation of European Sections of the Theosophical Society in Amsterdam. In July, Steiner begins the articles in *Luzifer-Gnosis* that will become *How to Know Higher Worlds* (CW 10) and *Cosmic Memory* (CW 11). In September, Annie Besant visits Germany. In December, Steiner lectures on Freemasonry. He mentions the High Grade Masonry derived from John Yarker and represented by Theodore Reuss and Karl Kellner as a blank slate "into which a good image could be placed."

1905: This year, Steiner ends his non-Theosophical lecturing activity. Supported by Marie von Sivers, his Theosophical lecturing—both in public and in the Theosophical Society—increases significantly: "The German Theosophical Movement is of exceptional importance." Steiner recommends reading, among others, Fichte, Jacob Boehme, and Angelus Silesius. He begins to introduce Christian themes into Theosophy. He also begins to work with doctors (Felix Peipers and Ludwig Noll). In July, he is in London for the Federation of European Sections, where he attends a lecture by Annie Besant: "I have seldom seen Mrs. Besant speak in so inward and heartfelt a manner…." "Through Mrs. Besant I have found the way to H.P. Blavatsky." September to October, he gives a course of thirty-one lectures for a small group of esoteric students. In October, the annual meeting of the German Section of the Theosophical Society, which still remains very small, takes place. Rudolf Steiner reports membership has risen from 121 to 377 members. In November, seeking to establish esoteric "continuity," Rudolf Steiner and Marie von Sivers participate in a "Memphis-Misraim" Masonic ceremony. They pay forty-five marks for membership. "Yesterday, you saw how little remains of former esoteric institutions." "We are dealing only with a 'framework'… for the present, nothing lies behind it. The occult powers have completely withdrawn."

1906: Expansion of Theosophical work. Rudolf Steiner gives about 245 lectures, only 44 of which take place in Berlin. Cycles are given in Paris, Leipzig, Stuttgart, and Munich. Esoteric work also intensifies. Rudolf Steiner begins writing *An Outline of Esoteric Science* (CW 13). In January, Rudolf Steiner receives permission (a patent) from the Great Orient of the Scottish A & A Thirty-Three Degree Rite of the Order of the Ancient Freemasons of the Memphis-Misraim Rite to direct a chapter under the name "Mystica Aeterna." This will become the "Cognitive-Ritual Section" (also called "Misraim Service") of the Esoteric School. (See: *Freemasonry and Ritual Work: The Misraim Service* (CW 265). During this time, Steiner also meets Albert Schweitzer. In May, he is in Paris, where he visits Edouard Schuré. Many Russians attend his lectures (including Konstantin Balmont, Dimitri Mereszkovski, Zinaida Hippius, and Maximilian Woloshin). He attends the General Meeting of the European Federation of the Theosophical Society, at which Col. Olcott is present for the last time. He spends the year's end in Venice and Rome, where he writes and works on his translation of H.P. Blavatsky's *Key to Theosophy*.

1907: Further expansion of the German Theosophical Movement according to the Rosicrucian directive to "introduce spirit into the world"—in education, in social questions, in art, and in science. In February, Col. Olcott dies in Adyar. Before he dies, Olcott indicates that "the Masters" wish Annie Besant to succeed him: much politicking ensues. Rudolf Steiner supports Besant's candidacy. April-May: preparations for the Congress of the Federation of European Sections of the Theosophical Society—the great, watershed Whitsun "Munich Congress," attended by Annie Besant and others. Steiner decides to separate Eastern and Western (Christian-Rosicrucian) esoteric schools. He takes his esoteric school out of the Theosophical Society (Besant and Rudolf Steiner are "in harmony" on this). Steiner makes his first lecture tours to Austria and Hungary. That summer, he is in Italy. In September, he visits Edouard Schuré, who will write the introduction to the French edition of *Christianity as Mystical Fact* in Barr, Alsace. Rudolf Steiner writes the autobiographical statement known as the "Barr Document." In *Luzifer–Gnosis*, "The Education of the Child" appears.

1908: The movement grows (membership: 1,150). Lecturing expands. Steiner makes his first extended lecture tour to Holland and Scandinavia, as well as visits to Naples and Sicily. Themes: St. John's Gospel, the Apocalypse, Egypt, science, philosophy, and logic. *Luzifer-Gnosis* ceases publication. In Berlin, Marie von Sivers (with Johanna Mücke (1864-1949) forms the *Philosophisch-Theosophisch* (after 1915 *Philosophisch-Anthroposophisch*) *Verlag* to publish Steiner's work. Steiner gives lecture cycles titled *The Gospel of St. John* (CW 103) and *The Apocalypse* (104).

1909: *An Outline of Esoteric Science* appears. Lecturing and travel continues. Rudolf Steiner's spiritual research expands to include the polarity of Lucifer and Ahriman; the work of great individualities in history; the Maitreya Buddha and the Bodhisattvas; spiritual economy (CW 109); the work of the spiritual hierarchies in heaven and on earth (CW 110). He also deepens and intensifies his research into the Gospels, giving lectures on the Gospel of St. Luke (CW 114) with the first mention of two Jesus children. Meets and becomes friends with Christian Morgenstern (1871-1914). In April, he lays the foundation stone for the Malsch model—the building that will lead to the first Goetheanum. In May, the International Congress of the Federation of European Sections of the Theosophical Society takes place in Budapest. Rudolf Steiner receives the Subba Row medal for *How to Know Higher Worlds*. During this time, Charles W. Leadbeater discovers Jiddu Krishnamurti (1895-1986) and proclaims him the future "world teacher," the bearer of the Maitreya Buddha and the "reappearing Christ." In October, Steiner delivers seminal lectures on "anthroposophy," which he will try, unsuccessfully, to rework over the next years into the unfinished work, *Anthroposophy (A Fragment)* (CW 45).

1910:   New themes: *The Reappearance of Christ in the Etheric* (CW 118); *The Fifth Gospel; The Mission of Folk Souls* (CW 121); *Occult History* (CW 126); the evolving development of etheric cognitive capacities. Rudolf Steiner continues his Gospel research with *The Gospel of St. Matthew* (CW 123). In January, his father dies. In April, he takes a month-long trip to Italy, including Rome, Monte Cassino, and Sicily. He also visits Scandinavia again. July-August, he writes the first mystery drama, *The Portal of Initiation* (CW 14). In November, he gives "psychosophy" lectures. In December, he submits "On the Psychological Foundations and Epistemological Framework of Theosophy" to the International Philosophical Congress in Bologna.

1911:   The crisis in the Theosophical Society deepens. In January, "The Order of the Rising Sun," which will soon become "The Order of the Star in the East," is founded for the coming world teacher, Krishnamurti. At the same time, Marie von Sivers, Rudolf Steiner's coworker, falls ill. Fewer lectures are given, but important new ground is broken. In Prague, in March, Steiner meets Franz Kafka (1883-1924) and Hugo Bergmann (1883-1975). In April, he delivers his paper to the Philosophical Congress. He writes the second mystery drama, *The Soul's Probation* (CW 14). Also, while Marie von Sivers is convalescing, Rudolf Steiner begins work on *Calendar 1912/1913*, which will contain the "Calendar of the Soul" meditations. On March 19, Anna (Eunike) Steiner dies. In September, Rudolf Steiner visits Einsiedeln, birthplace of Paracelsus. In December, Friedrich Rittelmeyer, future founder of the Christian Community, meets Rudolf Steiner. The *Johannes-Bauverein*, the "building committee," which would lead to the first Goetheanum (first planned for Munich), is also founded, and a preliminary committee for the founding of an independent association is created that, in the following year, will become the Anthroposophical Society. Important lecture cycles include *Occult Physiology* (CW 128); *Wonders of the World* (CW 129); *From Jesus to Christ* (CW 131). Other themes: esoteric Christianity; Christian Rosenkreutz; the spiritual guidance of humanity; the sense world and the world of the spirit.

1912:   Despite the ongoing, now increasing crisis in the Theosophical Society, much is accomplished: *Calendar 1912/1913* is published; eurythmy is created; both the third mystery drama, *The Guardian of the Threshold* (CW 14) and *A Way of Self-Knowledge* (CW 16) are written. New (or renewed) themes included life between death and rebirth and karma and reincarnation. Other lecture cycles: *Spiritual Beings in the Heavenly Bodies and in the Kingdoms of Nature* (CW 136); *The Human Being in the Light of Occultism, Theosophy, and Philosophy* (CW 137); *The Gospel of St. Mark* (CW 139); and *The Bhagavad Gita and the Epistles of Paul* (CW 142). On May 8, Rudolf Steiner celebrates White Lotus Day, H.P. Blavatsky's death day, which he had faithfully observed for the past decade, for the last time. In August, Rudolf Steiner suggests the "independent association" be called the "Anthroposophical Society." In September, the first eurythmy course takes place. In October, Rudolf Steiner declines recognition of a Theosophical Society lodge dedicated to the Star of the East and decides to expel all Theosophical Society members belonging to the order. Also, with Marie von Sivers, he first visits Dornach, near Basel, Switzerland, and they stand on the hill where the Goetheanum will be built. In November, a Theosophical Society lodge is opened by direct mandate from Adyar (Annie Besant). In December, a meeting of the German section occurs at which it is decided that belonging to the Order of the Star of the East is incompatible with membership in the Theosophical Society. December 28: informal founding of the Anthroposophical Society in Berlin.

1913: Expulsion of the German section from the Theosophical Society. February 2-3: Foundation meeting of the Anthroposophical Society. Board members include: Marie von Sivers, Michael Bauer, and Carl Unger. September 20: Laying of the foundation stone for the *Johannes Bau* (Goetheanum) in Dornach. Building begins immediately. The third mystery drama, *The Soul's Awakening* (CW 14), is completed. Also: *The Threshold of the Spiritual World* (CW 147). Lecture cycles include: *The Bhagavad Gita and the Epistles of Paul* and *The Esoteric Meaning of the Bhagavad Gita* (CW 146), which the Russian philosopher Nikolai Berdyaev attends; *The Mysteries of the East and of Christianity* (CW 144); *The Effects of Esoteric Development* (CW 145); and *The Fifth Gospel* (CW 148). In May, Rudolf Steiner is in London and Paris, where anthroposophical work continues.

1914: Building continues on the *Johannes Bau* (Goetheanum) in Dornach, with artists and coworkers from seventeen nations. The general assembly of the Anthroposophical Society takes place. In May, Rudolf Steiner visits Paris, as well as Chartres Cathedral. June 28: assassination in Sarajevo ("Now the catastrophe has happened!"). August 1: War is declared. Rudolf Steiner returns to Germany from Dornach—he will travel back and forth. He writes the last chapter of *The Riddles of Philosophy*. Lecture cycles include: *Human and Cosmic Thought* (CW 151); *Inner Being of Humanity between Death and a New Birth* (CW 153); *Occult Reading and Occult Hearing* (CW 156). December 24: marriage of Rudolf Steiner and Marie von Sivers.

1915: Building continues. Life after death becomes a major theme, also art. Writes: *Thoughts during a Time of War* (CW 24). Lectures include: *The Secret of Death* (CW 159); *The Uniting of Humanity through the Christ Impulse* (CW 165).

1916: Rudolf Steiner begins work with Edith Maryon (1872-1924) on the sculpture "The Representative of Humanity" ("The Group"—Christ, Lucifer, and Ahriman). He also works with the alchemist Alexander von Bernus on the quarterly *Das Reich*. He writes *The Riddle of Humanity* (CW 20). Lectures include:

Necessity and Freedom in World History and Human Action (CW 166); *Past and Present in the Human Spirit* (CW 167); *The Karma of Vocation* (CW 172); *The Karma of Untruthfulness* (CW 173).

1917:   Russian Revolution. The U.S. enters the war. Building continues. Rudolf Steiner delineates the idea of the "threefold nature of the human being" (in a public lecture March 15) and the "threefold nature of the social organism" (hammered out in May-June with the help of Otto von Lerchenfeld and Ludwig Polzer-Hoditz in the form of two documents titled *Memoranda*, which were distributed in high places). August-September: Rudolf Steiner writes *The Riddles of the Soul* (CW 20). Also: commentary on "The Chemical Wedding of Christian Rosenkreutz" for Alexander Bernus (*Das Reich*). Lectures include: *The Karma of Materialism* (CW 176); *The Spiritual Background of the Outer World: The Fall of the Spirits of Darkness* (CW 177).

1918:   March 18: peace treaty of Brest-Litovsk—"Now everything will truly enter chaos! What is needed is cultural renewal." June: Rudolf Steiner visits Karlstein (Grail) Castle outside Prague. Lecture cycle: *From Symptom to Reality in Modern History* (CW 185). In mid-November, Emil Molt, of the Waldorf-Astoria Cigarette Company, has the idea of founding a school for his workers' children.

1919:   Focus on the threefold social organism: tireless travel, countless lectures, meetings, and publications. At the same time, a new public stage of Anthroposophy emerges as cultural renewal begins. The coming years will see initiatives in pedagogy, medicine, pharmacology, and agriculture. January 27: threefold meeting: " We must first of all, with the money we have, found free schools that can bring people what they need." February: first public eurythmy performance in Zurich. Also: "Appeal to the German People" (CW 24), circulated March 6 as a newspaper insert. In April, *Towards Social Renewal* (CW 23) appears—"perhaps the most widely read of all books on politics appearing since the war." Rudolf Steiner is asked to undertake the "direction and leadership" of the school founded by the Waldorf-Astoria Company. Rudolf Steiner begins to talk about the "renewal" of education. May 30: a building is selected and purchased for the future Waldorf School. August-September, Rudolf Steiner gives a lecture course for Waldorf teachers, *The Foundations of Human Experience (Study of Man)* (CW 293). September 7: Opening of the first Waldorf School. December (into January): first science course, the *Light Course* (CW 320).

1920:   The Waldorf School flourishes. New threefold initiatives. Founding of limited companies *Der Kommende Tag* and *Futurum A.G.* to infuse spiritual values into the economic realm. Rudolf Steiner also focuses on the sciences. Lectures: *Introducing Anthroposophical Medicine* (CW 312); *The Warmth Course* (CW 321); *The Boundaries of Natural Science* (CW 322); *The Redemption of Thinking* (CW 74). February: Johannes Werner Klein—later a cofounder of the Christian Community—asks Rudolf Steiner about the possibility of a "religious renewal," a "Johannine church." In March, Rudolf Steiner gives the first course for doctors and medical students. In April, a divinity student asks Rudolf Steiner a second time about the possibility of religious renewal. September 27-October 16: anthroposophical "university course." December: lectures titled *The Search for the New Isis* (CW 202).

1921:   Rudolf Steiner continues his intensive work on cultural renewal, including the uphill battle for the threefold social order. "University" arts, scientific, theological, and medical courses include: *The Astronomy Course* (CW 323); *Observation, Mathematics, and Scientific Experiment* (CW 324); the *Second Medical Course* (CW 313); *Color*. In June and September-October, Rudolf Steiner also gives the first two "priests' courses" (CW 342 and 343). The "youth movement" gains momentum. Magazines are founded: *Die Drei* (January), and—under the editorship of Albert Steffen (1884-1963)—the weekly, *Das Goetheanum* (August). In February-March, Rudolf Steiner takes his first trip outside Germany since the war (Holland). On April 7, Steiner receives a letter regarding "religious renewal," and May 22-23, he agrees to address the question in a practical way. In June, the Klinical-Therapeutic Institute opens in Arlesheim under the direction of Dr. Ita Wegman. In August, the Chemical-Pharmaceutical Laboratory opens in Arlesheim (Oskar Schmiedel and Ita Wegman are directors). The Clinical Therapeutic Institute is inaugurated in Stuttgart (Dr. Ludwig Noll is director); also the Research Laboratory in Dornach (Ehrenfried Pfeiffer and Gunther Wachsmuth are directors). In November-December, Rudolf Steiner visits Norway.

1922: The first half of the year involves very active public lecturing (thousands attend); in the second half, Rudolf Steiner begins to withdraw and turn toward the Society—"The Society is asleep." It is "too weak" to do what is asked of it. The businesses—*Der Kommende Tag* and *Futura A.G.*—fail. In January, with the help of an agent, Steiner undertakes a twelve-city German lecture tour, accompanied by eurythmy performances. In two weeks he speaks to more than 2,000 people. In April, he gives a "university course" in The Hague. He also visits England. In June, he is in Vienna for the East-West Congress. In August-September, he is back in England for the Oxford Conference on Education. Returning to Dornach, he gives the lectures *Philosophy, Cosmology, and Religion* (CW 215), and gives the third priests' course (CW 344). On September 16, The Christian Community is founded. In October-November, Steiner is in Holland and England. He also speaks to the youth: *The Youth Course* (CW 217). In December, Steiner gives lectures titled *The Origins of Natural Science* (CW 326), and *Humanity and the World of Stars: The Spiritual Communion of Humanity* (CW 219). December 31: Fire at the Goetheanum, which is destroyed.

1923: Despite the fire, Rudolf Steiner continues his work unabated. A very hard year. Internal dispersion, dissension, and apathy abound. There is conflict—between old and new visions—within the society. A wake-up call is needed, and Rudolf Steiner responds with renewed lecturing vitality. His focus: the spiritual context of human life; initiation science; the course of the year; and community building. As a foundation for an artistic school, he creates a series of pastel sketches. Lecture cycles: *The Anthroposophical Movement; Initiation Science* (CW 227) (in England at the Penmaenmawr Summer School); *The Four Seasons and the Archangels* (CW 229); *Harmony of the Creative Word* (CW 230); *The Supersensible Human* (CW 231), given in Holland for the founding of the Dutch society. On November 10, in response to the failed Hitler-Ludendorf putsch in Munich, Steiner closes his Berlin residence and moves the *Philosophisch-Anthroposophisch Verlag* (Press) to Dornach. On December 9, Steiner begins the serialization of his *Autobiography: The Course of My Life* (CW 28) in *Das Goetheanum*. It will continue to appear weekly, without a break, until his death. Late December-early January: Rudolf Steiner refounds the Anthroposophical Society (about 12,000 members internationally) and takes over its leadership. The new board members are: Marie Steiner, Ita Wegman, Albert Steffen, Elizabeth Vreede, and Guenther Wachsmuth. (See *The Christmas Meeting for the Founding of the General Anthroposophical Society* (CW 260). Accompanying lectures: *Mystery Knowledge and Mystery Centers* (CW 232); *World History in the Light of Anthroposophy* (CW 233). December 25: the Foundation Stone is laid (in the hearts of members) in the form of the "Foundation Stone Meditation."

1924: January 1: having founded the Anthroposophical Society and taken over its leadership, Rudolf Steiner has the task of "reforming" it. The process begins with a weekly newssheet ("What's Happening in the Anthroposophical Society") in which Rudolf Steiner's "Letters to Members" and "Anthroposophical Leading Thoughts" appear (CW 26). The next step is the creation of a new esoteric class, the "first class" of the "University of Spiritual Science" (which was to have been followed, had Rudolf Steiner lived longer, by two more advanced classes). Then comes a new language for Anthroposophy—practical, phenomenological, and direct; and Rudolf Steiner creates the model for the second Goetheanum. He begins the series of extensive "karma" lectures (CW 235-40); and finally, responding to needs, he creates two new initiatives: biodynamic agriculture and curative education. After the middle of the year, rumors begin to circulate regarding Steiner's health. Lectures: January-February, *Anthroposophy* (CW 234); February: *Tone Eurythmy* (CW 278); June: *The Agriculture Course* (CW 327); June-July: Speech [?] Eurythmy (CW 279); *Curative Education* (CW 317); August: (England, "Second International Summer School"), *Initiation Consciousness: True and False Paths in Spiritual Investigation* (CW 243); September: *Pastoral Medicine* (CW 318). On September 26, for the first time, Rudolf Steiner cancels a lecture. On September 28, he gives his last lecture. On September 29, he withdraws to his studio in the carpenter's shop; now he is definitively ill. Cared for by Ita Wegman, he continues working, however, and writing the weekly installments of his *Autobiography* and *Letters to the Members/ Leading Thoughts* (CW 26).

1925: Rudolf Steiner, while continuing to work, continues to weaken. He finishes *Extending Practical Medicine* (CW 27) with Ita Wegman.

On March 30, around ten in the morning, Rudolf Steiner dies.